SECRETS TO PRICING AND DISTRIBUTION

Ebook, Print and Direct Sales

MAGGIE MCVAY LYNCH

Once you have books to sell, you need to get them into readers' hands. Uninitiated authors may simply follow the vendor's prompts, load their book, and then hope for the best. However, the career author knows that each vendor has its own methods of promoting books and providing special author opportunities to gain readership. You want to take advantage of these nuances in order to maximize your profits and discoverability.

This book helps prepares you to effectively tackle all the metadata required to load your books into any vendor's system.

You will learn how to:

- Maximize the use of metadata across multiple platforms to enhance discoverability.
- Write compelling book blurbs for each title, focusing on "reader cookies" and marketing.
- Identify appropriate categories for your books.
- Select effective keywords based on search algorithms.
- Load your book to the top ebook distribution vendors: Amazon, Barnes and Noble, Kobo, and Apple.
- Setup and use your author profile around the world to maximize discoverability according to each vendor's rules and reach.
- Evaluate aggregators and how they can help you with distribution to the big four vendors and/or to others beyond the big four.
- Work with bookstores to help them sell both your e-book and print titles.
- Set up an online and in-person direct sales mechanism for your e-books

Copyright © 2017 by **Maggie McVay Lynch**

All rights reserved. No part of this publication may be reproduced, distributed or transmitted in any form or by any means, without prior written permission.

Windtree Press

Hillsboro, Oregon

http://windtreepress.com

Cover Design by Christy Keerins

https://coveredbyclkeerins.com/

Secrets to Pricing and Distribution: Ebooks, Print, and Direct Sales / Maggie McVay Lynch. -- 1st ed.

Print ISBN 978-19449738-0-3

Ebook ISBN 978-19449738-1-0

United States of America

❦ Created with Vellum

To my husband, Jim, who has supported my writing career from the day we met 18 years ago. He has been my rock through crazy writing binges, through my complaints about the changing state of publishing, and through the many times I am away from home retreating at the beach, presenting workshops, attending conferences, or just talking on the phone with a writer who needs a little extra encouragement.

Chapter One
DEFINITIONS

Whenever you are entering a new world, it is important that you understand what the typical words used (often called jargon) mean in that world. In this book we are talking about distribution in both print and ebook and how to get discovered among the millions of books out there. So let's start with some definitions that we will be using throughout the chapters of the book.

Discoverability – This is the "buzzword" of the past five years. It refers to how a book is found (discovered) by a reader. In 2016, according to Bowker, nearly a million new titles were published. And that is probably low, because Bowker can only track the books that have an associated ISBN. For authors who publish only in ebook, many do not have an ISBN because most ebook vendors don't require them. This is your competition with each new book coming out. In addition, you are competing with all the books available that have come out before.

Before becoming "visible," however, as obvious as it might seem, a book has to be found. That is what "discoverability" tries to address. That process is one that both big NY publishers and small Indie publishers have not yet cracked. But you will learn some techniques for enhancing your books chance for being discovered.

Distribution – The Distributor acts as the link between publisher and retailer or consumer in cases where the publisher does not want to be involved in shipping books and collecting money from readers. The distributor receives orders from retailers or consumers, ships books, and handles all the money. This is normally done on a commission basis. Amazon is a distributor. Amazon takes your self-published book (You are the publisher) and through an agreement with you makes it available via all of their outlets. For this service they **charge you a percentage of your sales** ranging from 30% to 65%. When you get a 70% royalty from Amazon, then Amazon is taking a 30% commission. When you get a 35% royalty from Amazon (because of pricing or not being in Select), then Amazon is taking a 65% commission. The same goes for other distributors: Kobo, Apple, B&N, Google, etc.

For print books, the two big distributors for Indies are Createspace and Ingram. Again, each distributor takes a chunk of money from you. In the case of Createspace, their commission is 40% on your print-on-demand (POD) book. In the case of Ingram, their commission is 35% on POD. Print-on-demand has been a life saver for Indies because you don't have to put any money upfront to make sure your books are available in print. If you want to do print runs for mass market, like major publishers do, then you must pay a printer up front for your books and there is usually a minimum order required (e.g., 500 or 1,000 books).

A distributor usually handles books from several publishers. Large national publishers may do their own distribution, or own a separate distribution company. The publisher (You) is still responsible for marketing the book, that is, creating a demand for it through advertising, promotion, author tours, etc. The distributor merely fills the orders.

Metadata – The dictionary definition of this is "data about data." For our purposes metadata is any piece of information about you, your book, your writing work. It begins with a collection of attributes—ISBN, title, author, copyright year, price, subject category, etc. This title-level metadata started with library catalogs. But beyond that it is your book description, your character descriptions, your blogs, your Facebook posts, your tweets—in other words every piece of information you make publicly available is now metadata.

Producer (Book Producer) - A book producer handles any or all aspects of putting a book together and getting it printed (and some times distributed). This includes editing, cover design, typesetting, image preparation, digital page composition, obtaining printer quotes, and working with the printer. Some Book Producers also handle the uploading of your finished books to various distributors.

Usually the publisher (You) performs these functions, but there are companies (Book Baby is one such legitimate company) that produce books for indie publishers on a contract basis. This may be small press publishers as well as self-publishers. The important thing to remember is that the producer is really a contractor. The producer does not own the books or the copyright. You, as the publisher, are paying for a contracted producer to provide this service for you. After your book is produced, printed or loaded to distributors, it is still up to the publisher (YOU) to handle the marketing and receive all income from sales.

Book producers work in two different payment schemes: 1) You pay for everything up front (this usually ranges from $500-$1,500 per book; or 2) You pay some fee up front and, if the producer loaded the book to distributors for you, the producer then takes a commission from every sale. This means that if that producer loads your book to Amazon for you, and that book would normally get a 70% royalty. Then you will likely only get 55% because the producer will take their 15% out before paying you what is owed.

Publisher - The publisher is the person, organization, or company that finances the book and controls the editing, designing, printing, and marketing of it. The publisher is the risk taker and owns the physical and digital books. When you self-publish **YOU are the publisher**—not Amazon, Not Kobo, Not B&N or Apple. They are all distributors. You are the publisher.

If you are paying for the production and printing of your book, you are the publisher. Anyone else involved, regardless of what they refer to themselves as, is merely a contractor. Cover designers, editors, formatters, etc. are all contractors.

Search Engine Optimization (SEO) – Search Engine Optimization is the process of making your book, your brand, your name more visible whenever someone does an organic search. Every business wants to be in the top rankings. They want their website or product to turn up on the first page of search results on Google or other search engines.

SEO involves a number of adjustments to the HTML of individual Web pages to achieve a high search ranking. First, the title of the page must include relevant information about the page. Then there are ways to enhance that description with what is called META tags. These are special HTML codes that can really distinguish your site or product from the rest of the pile. The META tags that most search engines read for books are the description, keywords, and categories. You don't have to know HTML to create metadata. Every time you fill out a form at a distributor or create a blog or post something to the web, you are creating metadata and HTML coding is being done behind the scenes. Even if you don't know how to do this HTML tagging yourself, you need to understand the purpose of it. Every distributor uses these tags in order to best feature all products on their site and to get higher in search rankings.

Keywords – Keywords are words or phrases that describe content. They can be used as metadata to describe images, text documents, and Web pages. A user may "tag" pictures or text files with keywords that are relevant to their content. Later on, these files may be searched using keywords, which can make finding files much easier.

The role of keywords in searches has been greatly reduced, though they are still important. Search engines could crawl sites and, if the keywords were accurate, serve those sites up as search results. However, people began abusing the keyword metadata in an attempt to show up higher in searches, and even to rank in completely unrelated searches. For this reason, keywords are no longer a primary factor in SEO. There is a combination of factors that make a difference in rankings in order to try to keep out the "marketing" abusers.

Chapter Two

THE IMPORTANCE OF PRICING COMPETITIVELY WITHIN YOUR DISTRIBUTION NETWORK

I struggled with whether to begin with Pricing or Distribution. I decided that Pricing would go first because you will need to have established your price when you load your book to any distributor. A good understanding of pricing strategies is critical to the indie author in order to be competitive in todays market.

The first thing to realize about pricing is that there is absolutely no way you can price your book at the real value you perceive it is worth. If you took a year to write your book—even at minimum wage—it may mean that you've invested the equivalent of about $8,000 of your time (this is assuming you worked on it 20 hours per week at $8.00 per hour). Then if you add to that costs of getting a professional cover, paying for editing, or other contracted services, it can easily be $10,000. How do you come up with a price that reflects all that work?

The answer is, you can't. Whatever price you might think your book is worth (e.g., maybe $9-$10 per copy), it is likely no one will pay for it. Pricing is one of the important pieces that can draw people to give you a chance or immediately turn them away.

A mistake that many authors make—both with print and ebook pricing—is trying to match the pricing that big, traditional publishers are using. The reality is you can't afford to compete with big publishers. First, is you can't afford the upfront costs. Second, you can't afford the potential losses if you price too high or too low.

On the print size, publishers are doing print runs in the thousands in order to keep the cost down and still make a good profit. Big publishers can afford to price a mass market book at $5.99 because they did a print run of 25,000 books that cost them $50,000. It is likely that the typical POD novel costs between $3.00 and $4.00 to the indie author. That is before any commissions taken by distributors (e.g., Create Space taking 40% of retail). You simply can't get your book to that price.

On the ebook side, publishers often price ebooks at a rate equivalent to mass market ($5.99-$9.99) depending on the popularity of the author. They do this because they prefer that readers buy print books. They are trying to dissuade readers from choosing ebooks. Again, most authors can't afford to price their books like this because they are not popular enough to command that pricing. They are competing with average prices of $2.99-$4.99.

For most authors, print pricing tends to be dictated by the cost of the book to the author and the distribution fees and commissions. Using the calclators provided by both Amazon and Ingram, you can quickly see that to make even a modest profit, requires most indie novels to be sold in the $12-$18 range. It may be possible to get a novella down to the $8-$9 range.

The price for ebooks, on the other hand, is significantly more varied. Unlike printing costs, delivering a digital file is close to free for distributors. So, the indie author only needs to take into consideration the commissions charged by the distributor.

The one exception to this is Amazon. Amazon does charge a "delivery fee" for every book based on the size of the file. The minimum charge is one cent. Though it varies from country to country, the charge is approximately 15 cents per megabyte. The typical novel, all words with no images except the cover, costs about five cents. If you use images (logos, header images, special divider images) then costs go up and can typically average around 15 cents per book.

However, nonfiction books—particularly if they have a lot of images, charts, tables—can cost as much as $1.00 depending on the size of the file. Some of this can be alleviated with better formatting and compressing image files.

Assuming the delivery costs are minimal across multiple vendors, how does an author decide what is a fair price for an ebook? Some authors set prices based on the length of the book. For example, a 10,000 word title might be 99 cents, a novella (15K-40K) might be $2.99, and novels are from $3.99 to $6.99. The problem with this is that it is not the value YOU perceive is correct. Instead it is the value your READER believes is accurate.

Readers tend to value books based on certain factors:

1. **Do they already know and love you?** If they are already hooked on your books or a series, they are likely to pay more for the next book. If they don't know you, they are unlikely to even give you a try unless they perceive your book as a bargain.
2. **How does your price compare to the majority of books similar to yours?** There are certain genres that average higher in price than others. For example, romance books tend to be in the $2.99 to $3.99 range unless the author is a bestseller. This means, even if you have a 90K book, you probably can't compete above $3.99. On the other hand a thriller may be able to command $4.99 just because thriller readers see that value. Even with $4.99 being the average, there are still a lot of bestselling thriller authors who price their books at $3.99.
3. **Is the book a bestseller and everyone is talking about it?** If you are fortunate enough to have a book that already has a lot of buzz, then you can command higher prices. Most indie authors—particularly those with only a couple of books out—are not in this fortunate circumstance yet.

Strategies for Determining Price

First, you have to determine your goal with a particular title. Are you looking to get more readers or more sales? If you are like me you want both. However, the pricing strategies differ depending on your answer and on where you are in your career.

If you want more sales, you have to evaluate if you can sell six times more books at 99 cents than at $6.99. Certainly, priced at $6.99 each book yields you more profit. However, if very few readers choose to pay that price, it doesn't get you more money in the end. On the other hand, a lot more people MAY take a chance at a new author whose book is only 99 cents. But, to make the some money you need to sell a lot more books—engage a lot more readers. For new or unknown authors, a lower price may help draw in new readers.

If you determined that your goal was to focus on getting more readers, and not worrying as much about making money, then the priority should be getting the price as low as possible. Remember, whatever the price it is not set in stone. One of the techniques used by indie authors is to change price (or have discounts) from time to time in order to get more exposure. If you can get a burst of sales at the lower price, it ups your sales rank for the category. That automatically means it is getting shown to potential customers more often. Then you can return to the "normal" price again and ride that sales rank for a while.

What is a good middle ground? Where to start experimenting with price.

Initial book pricing is discussed in a good amount of detail in the *Secrets Every Author Should Know: Indie Publishing Basics* book. So, I'm going to summarize the key points in this section.

The best place to start is to evaluate the competition. What genre is your book? How many readers are in that genre? Where is the book being sold—country, store/vendor, time of year your book is released.

When it comes to determining a price, you really need to think of your book as a widget. For example, a house in New York City costs more than the same house in Gary, Indiana. That house is also listed for more in the spring and summer when more people want to move than it is in the winter. A little black, shift dress by Chanel (a name brand designer) costs significantly more than a dress that looks exactly the same made by Susie's Home Sewing. How does your book compare to top sellers? What is the same and different?

Too often authors look at the top sellers in their genre and think: "My book is just as good, if not better, than that one." It may be true; but that doesn't mean a reader will pay you the same price for your book that they pay for the name brand author. A brand name author comes with a known experience expectation. An unknown author has no guarantees and, in fact, is often compared to any other unknown author the reader tried in the past. If the reader has tried unknown authors and had a good experience, she may be more likely to give you a try. If the experience was bad, she is more likely to pass up your book unless something (like price) makes the attempt less costly. This is why free and 99 cents are so popular. A reader thinks: "It's only 99 cents. If it's a bad book, I'm not out much money."

When a reader sees your book, her first concern is what will be the *experience* of reading that book. If it is a fiction book, will the experience match my reader cookies—expectations for characters, emotion, adventure, fright or feel good moments? If it is a nonfiction book, will I learn something I don't already know that makes my time worthwhile?

Go to a few vendor sites (Amazon is one of the easiest to navigate) and search for bestsellers in your genre. Make a list of what is alike and different between those books and your own. If you have books already out there, you can make the assumption that your new book will do as well as past books. If this is your first book, assume that your book will do as well as the average one book author. Here is an example of one of my lists for a recent fiction book release.

	Bestseller Book	My Book
Author Ranking	Top 100	Maybe 10,000 on launch, falling to 30-50K soon after
Number of Reviews	Over 300	Probably 25-30
Cover Quality	Professional	Professional
Blurb	Good, draws reader in	Good, draws reader in
Length	230	290
Series #	3rd book	4th book
Price	$4.99	???

Taking into account all of the above, I doubt I can price at $4.99 and pull in enough money. The question is whether I should price at $2.99 or $3.99. I decide to do $3.99 because my book is longer, it is further along in a series that has a decent following, and the majority of authors in the genre price full length novels at either $2.99 or $3.99 if they aren't bestsellers.

The good news is the price is not set in stone. You can change it at any time. Just make sure that when you change your price, you have good reason to do so (e.g., special marketing) or data gathered over a significant period of time suggests a different price.

NOTE: *a few days or a couple weeks is NOT a significant period of time. It takes a new title a minimum of 4-6 weeks to get the metadata for searches and ranking populated to all the vendors and start building a history of views, clicks, and sales.*

Now that I've been self-publishing since 2011, I've built a basic pricing scheme I use when first launching a book.

Longer short stories – between 4,000 and 8,500 words are priced at 99 cents. I don't put up stories shorter than 4K. These rarely sell but having placed a value on them it works to my advantage when bundling into a collection.

Novelettes – 8,500-15,000 words are also priced at 99 cents. Some better known authors may push these to $1.99 or $2.99 but I haven't found those higher prices work for me.

Novellas – 15,000-40,000 words are $2.99. This is a popular length in several genres (romance, mystery, horror) and with the combination of downward pricing pressure and more readers looking for short works, the $2.99 price point seems fair.

Novels – 40,000 to 90,000 words are $3.99. Some authors break this into short novels (40-65K) and long novels (70-100K) with the longer novels at $4.99. I haven't found that novel length makes a difference in pricing. It makes a difference in expectation based on genre norms (e.g., historical novels tend to be longer than contemporary novels), but not necessarily on the reader's view of pricing value.

Having these basic rules of pricing for my fiction work makes it much easier for me to know what I'm going to do each time. Of course, as the publishing landscape changes my pricing may change. I look at my entire inventory about every six months and re-evaluate prices based on my goals and what the market will bear for that year. I also flex pricing for specific marketing goals (e.g., first book in series discounted to draw reader in).

Flex Pricing Based on Your Genre and Market

The publishing landscape changes from year to year. In the last two years (2015 and 2016) there has been more downward pressure on pricing than there were in previous years (2011-2014). Part of this is due to the increased competition from some big, traditional publishers who are trying different pricing strategies now instead of automatically pricing mass market and ebooks the same. Another part of downward pricing pressure is simply the competition for discoverability among millions of books. If you have not changed your ebook price for a couple of years and sales are not doing well, consider re-evaluating what that price should be based on today's market.

All books are a product. If you look at products in any other retail store, you know that prices never remain static. There are always sales, discounts, and price reductions. In addition, the same product may be priced differently in different stores depending on its location and customer demographic.

Retail pricing is fluid and flexible, and in the case of ebooks, it is very easy to change the selling price and experiment with a range of prices and pricing strategies, which may help to increase your visibility and thus your sales. Also consider that book pricing in another country may be very different than pricing in the U.S.

Five Ebook Pricing Strategies to Consider When Troubleshooting a Sales Problem

1. Increase your price. This may sound odd if you are struggling with sales. However, a higher price can create a perception that your book is a better product. Because of the plethora of books available for free or at 99 cents, a number of readers have built a perception that those are less polished books or not as good as traditional books.

Try increasing your price by a dollar. Watch it for two or three months and see if it makes a difference. Sales at a higher price will increase your ranking much faster than sales at 99 cents.

2. Price differently for different countries. Expectations within a country may differ significantly from the U.S. Most distributors automatically translate pricing to current currency exchange rates. However, that doesn't necessarily mean you should leave it at the converted price. For example, some researchers have found that the sweet spot for U.S. fiction ebook sales is between $2.99 and $4.99. However, in the U.K. ebook buyers are far more reluctant to buy ebooks priced over £1.99 (approximately $2.70 US) prior to VAT being added. So, if your book is priced at $3.99 in the U.S. the translated number for the UK is £3.04, significantly higher than the £1.99 threshold.

On the other hand in some European countries, the perception is if the book is less than the equivalent of $3.99 that it is a trash book—not worth taking the time to try. Do the same research on book pricing in other countries before assuming your translated U.S. price will result in similar sales.

3. Make the first book in a series very inexpensive. If you have published a series, consider pricing the first book in the series at 99 cents to hook new readers, and then set each subsequent title in steps of $1.00 more up to $3.99 or $4.99 (depending on genre) for the latest title in the series. Many authors with series price the most recent release high and then lower the previous book's pricing.

Of course, this also depends on the number of books you put out every year. If you are putting out a new book every month in a series, then lowering the price for the previous month's book may not make sense. There is still significant chance's that when your new release comes out, new readers will go back and read the previous books. However, if you are only putting out one book a year in a series, it may make sense to lower the pricing for the previous year's release.

4. Always make sure you have a paperback book available (even if you never sell one). Amazon always shows all versions of a book on the page. At Amazon it is particularly striking because Amazon shows the print book price with a slash through it in comparison to the significantly lower ebook price. It makes it look like a discount or special sale price. So, why not take advantage of that and make all your ebooks look like a bigger discount?

Note: Some books don't make sense to have a paperback copy created (e.g., short stories or short non-fiction books under 50 pages). However, I always make a print on demand (POD) version of any book over 75 pages. I'll often pad out shorter works with a preview of the first chapters of a related book to at least make enough pages for a spine big enough to have the book name and author printed (that takes a minimum of 125 pages).

5. Increase the price before your free ebook days. If you have decided to be exclusive to Amazon, using KDP Select, then consider increasing your price for a couple weeks before doing your five free days. Set your price to $3.99 or $4.99 to make your free ebook offering look like a bigger discount. Amazon will show the previous price of the book when it goes free. But you need some time on the market with at least one sale at that increased price.

TIP: This can also work in reverse for you. If you have a book at a discount, say 99 cents, that generated a lot of sales, it will retain your new higher ranking when changing the price. Consider, when you first put it back to normal pricing consider going a dollar higher than your previous normal price (e.g., $4.99 instead of $3.99) for a month. You may be pleasantly surprised at the result.

However, aising the price past the norm ONLY works if you had a significant number of downloads at the lower 99 cent price (e.g., 200+).

Summary

Don't be afraid to experiment with pricing. However, you also need to give it time, particularly if you are just starting out with your first book or your second or third book. Once you've set a "normal" price, you need to leave it there for at least one to two months to see how it works.

Far too many authors want immediate results and if the book hasn't started selling significantly at $2.99 they immediately drop it to 99 cents which changes the algorithm for ranking and provides not only less money overall but less percentage of price paid (35% instead of 70%). Dropping below $2.99 should be done carefully and with a good plan for capitalizing on that discount to make it worthwhile.

There are many factors that go into discoverability. Pricing is only one of them. Before making a quick change, be sure to check on the other parts of your book packaging. Reread the section on "Why Books Don't Sell" in the *Secrets Every Author Should Know: Indie Publishing Basics* book.

Also be sure to check out the section on pricing as it relates to launches and ongoing marketing in the book *Secrets to Effective Marketing: It's More Than "Buy My Book"*.

Chapter Three
DISTRIBUTION BASICS

Once you have books to sell, you need to get them into readers' hands. Uninitiated authors may simply follow the vendor's prompts, load their book, and then hope for the best. However, the career author knows that each vendor has its own methods of promoting books and providing special author opportunities to gain readership. You want to take advantage of these nuances in order to maximize your profits and discoverability.

This section prepares you to effectively tackle all the metadata required to load your books into any vendor's system. Getting discovered within a vendor's catalog relies on hundreds—or thousands in the case of Amazon—of metrics that they use to present the book the customer most likely wants to see. Though I can't cover all the different metrics that figure into the Amazon algorithm, what I can do is tell you about the five most important ones that are searched and impact rankings with a significant weight on metadata.

- Your Book Title
- Your Book Blurb
- The categories you select for your book
- The keywords you use

- Clicks to buy and clicks to view (sales and almost-sales)

Your Book Title

I don't know about you, but I know my book title before I even start writing it. Also, I'm a huge fan of one or two word titles. I love it when the title is able to reflect everything I want about the themes of the book, the mood, and the underlying character emotions. I feel pretty smug when it all comes together.

Unfortunately, metadata and reader cookies don't give one wit about my perfect titles. For example, my Contemporary Romance book is titled *Undertones*. Without any other cues—couple on the cover, subtitle, or genre—that title says absolutely nothing that would draw a romance reader to the book. I hate to admit it but there are really good reasons so many romance books have words like love, desire, passion, baby, duke, billionaire, etc. in the title. Each of those words gives a cue to the reader what type of romance the book will be. It's like someone standing in the bookstore saying: "Come over here, you'll like this book because it has LOVE in the title. You like to read about *love*, don't you?"

Now, you might think that I went out and changed all my titles to contain those words. Ummm...No. I LIKE my titles and I'm stubborn. But when I set up my next romance series, you better believe I'm going to consider some of those keywords in my title or subtitle.

Because I'm stubbornly not changing my past titles, what I can do to improve searches and increase metadata information, is to put some of those key words in other places, like:

- **A subtitle.** Undertones: A hot contemporary romance.
- **Weave it into the series title**—A Sweetwater Canyon *Romance.*
- **Pull it out of a review and feature it with my blurb**.

"Love abounds in this book of friendship, coming of age, and finding a happily ever after."
- **Interview myself** and put that interview at the bottom of my book description. It appears after the *read more* link, but all that information is still metadata and still getting mined by search engines.
- And, of course, I can use those words in my **keywords.**

If you can hit those "reader cookie" words in everything—the title, the blurb, the categories, and the keywords—it's like finding Willy Wonka's Golden Ticket. The more hits, the better chance of finding your reader.

Writing the Best Blurbs to Maximize Discoverability

There are all kinds of books and workshops on writing a book blurb. Having a good book blurb, or back cover blurb, is very important to selling the book. That usually consists of some combination of: the hook; setting or atmosphere; emotion; and payoff. When you write blurbs to maximize discoverability you have to think about "above the fold" and "below the fold." The fold means before the reader/buyer needs to scroll down. The most important part of your blurb is "above the fold"—on the page without scrolling and captures everything the reader needs to know to draw them in and want to learn more.

See the two screenshots below on two different vendors. Notice where the blurb cuts off and a link to read more is presented. Though the same text description and spacing was presented to both, it is beneficial to me to change that when doing the Amazon blurb because the amount of text that is shown is minimal and I don't want to waste good real estate with blank lines.

Amazon Blurb Sample

Apple iBookstore Blurb Sample

That space before you scroll is really variable depending on what type of device the reader is using. On a desktop computer with a 20" screen you have 300-400 words. On a typical tablet you have about 250 words. On a phone (and a lot of people read and look for books on their phones) you have about 100 words. This means you REALLY want to put the most important stuff in the first 100 words. And the second most in the second 100 words.

Finally, if/when your reader scrolls down (which 80% will NOT do), the rest of your info can go there. Don't worry it's still picked up by search algorithms even if your reader never sees it.

If you think 100 words is too short, I have news. When it comes to blog posts, web sites, and other places you also need to capture your entire novel in 40 words and even in 140 characters, including spaces, for a Tweet. That is really hard, but really critical. Because the web works in small bits of information delivered quickly, when people are scanning and browsing, they do not take time to read that 250 word blurb or 400 word blurb—at least not until your 140 character one has intrigued them enough to click to the next level.

What is it that makes someone read a blurb and then click to learn more? The answer is "reader cookies." That is that the blurb delivers on something the reader wants. Just like a cookie delivers a special taste when you are looking for something sweet and delicious, or comfortable, or maybe even spicy and surprising.

Think about eating that cookie. What is your favorite kind? Chocolate chip? Macadamia nut? Peanut butter? Jalapeno chili with a dust of sugar? Or just a plain sugar cookie? There are hundreds of cookie recipes, and there are also hundreds of different ways that readers look at a blurb. And the same reader may want a different kind of blurb depending on her mood, what her friends have been talking about, or what type of book was assigned in a class.

I know that when I'm feeling down about my world, I go looking for a suspense novel where it's going to be exciting but I know the bad guy will get his comeuppance and love will triumph over all. When I'm in a good mood, I don't need that kind of entertainment. Instead I go looking for something that will make me think and question and wonder what it is like to live in a completely unique environment—a particular kind of fantasy or SF novel.

At this point most authors are holding their head in their hands now and saying, "But I can't possibly meet every reader's needs at the moment she is looking! I can't possibly speak to every mood of a reader." And that is exactly right. You can't.

The first, and most important truth about writing blurbs, and discoverability as a whole, is that you can't please every reader and you shouldn't try. Instead you need to carefully narrow the audience for your book and then write directly to that reader and only that reader. Because, when you do that you, then you will know exactly what their "reader cookies" are and what the recipe is to make them want to come back for another bite and another and another.

Okay, I Know My Reader. What's the Recipe for the Cookies?

You have to develop the recipe. And that recipe will help you write the best blurbs ever. You do that by asking some questions of your reader.

1. **What will draw your reader into the story the quickest?** What is that reader looking for the most? This is called the hook. If your reader wants high-powered suspense, then your hook must present that suspense. If your reader wants a wounded hero, then you better present that wound first. If your reader wants a small town atmosphere, then you lead with that.
2. **What type of emotion, or non-emotion, does your reader want?** In romance novels, readers want to know there is a strong love story but also that it's not going to be easy to get there. They want to see the conflict/the fight. In some Science Fiction stories, the emotion may be non-existent or emerging as in a robot story. Or the intellectual exercise may be the most important thing for that reader. You need to concisely present the emotion as part of your blurb—the emotional connection that your reader wants.
3. **What is the intrigue? The promise you are making to your reader?** This simultaneously tells your reader what the payoff could be, without revealing it. It says: "If you stay with me you'll get everything you want and more." It's a contract between you and the reader. If you don't deliver on that

promise in the book, you will get some bad reviews and that reader may not try you again. A reader looks at the blurb and makes assumptions about what kind of book it will be. She buys the book based on a very short but intriguing promise that met her specific "cookie needs" at that moment.

What Types of Blurbs are There and Why?

There are three types of blurbs used in metadata: 1) Basic long form (100 words maximum); 2) Search engine two line descriptor (usually 40-60 words); and 3) Tag line descriptor (120-150 characters, including spaces). Each one serves a different purpose and is used in different places. But all three must have the three important elements—the hook, the emotion, and the promise. It gets more difficult to deliver all three of those as your word count gets smaller, but you really need to learn to do this.

The basic blurb is sometimes referred to as the long description. This is the one you load to all distributors and use in any long-form posting (e.g., blogs, articles, newsletter description, etc.). However, even this blurb is not your normal back cover 250-400 word blurb. Yes, most vendors will allow you to load that big 400 word behemoth. They do that because that's what so many indie authors demanded. However, the problem is that most consumers won't read it. Remember, they are scanning, browsing. They don't want to take a lot of time to read each blurb they want to make a decision and move on in order to process as many potential purchases as possible before making a decision. So, if you load that big long back cover blurb you already have a problem.

So the basic blurb should be close to 100 words or so. Also, in some venues—like guest posts or newsletter articles—you are severely limited in space. So this basic 100 word blurb is good for those venues as well.

The short description (the 40-60 word blurb). Whenever you put in search terms in Google or some other search engine, the link comes up with a very short, one to two line descriptor. Again the browsing, scanning consumer is reading those short descriptions and making a decision whether to click on the link or not. If you didn't provide a short description, then what appears there is the first 40-60 words of your blurb.

If your longer blurb began with a beautiful, atmospheric description but didn't get to the hook until the 61st word, or the emotion until the 75th word, or the promise until the 100th+ word then none of that appears and you have already lost a potential click.

The tag line descriptor (120-150 characters). Think of this as the vendor equivalent of a Google search. Different vendor catalogs have a restricted description that ends up to be closer to 20-30 words. The actual limitation is bits—sometimes thought of as characters and spaces. Similar to what you are allowed in a Tweet. Some people also call this tag line descriptor the "elevator pitch".

How can you provide the hook, the emotion, and the promise in 120 characters? The key is to think on themes and emotion, no plot. Once you have this down, it can be used effectively in lots of places.

- It can be the first line in your short description—something to catch the reader's attention.
- It can be used as a tweet with your cover.
- It can be used in ads, memes, and other social media implementation to get engagement.

Then you know it will come up absolutely everywhere and be cross-matched. It needs to be memorable but still provide the full function of a blurb.

Example: Let me give you an example from my own work. I'm going to show you before and after examples of the original back cover blurb to the "basic 100 word blurb" and then what the two shorter versions are. This is from the first book in my YA Fantasy series, <u>Chameleon: The Awakening</u>.

Initial published back cover blurb (257 words).
No identity. That's what it's like to be a human chameleon, and sixteen-year-old Camryn Painter wonders if she'll ever figure out who the real Camryn is—or should be. Just looking at someone else will cause her body to change into that person. Her parents called it her gift. She calls it her curse.

Then Ohar, a man with impossibly good looks and an ethereal manner offers her a way to claim her birthright by joining the Mazikeen as part of the Forest People. He says she is "the chosen" of the Forest People. The prophecy indicates her powers are beyond any others and she will save their world.

Camryn had always loved the Redwoods at her back door. The stories her mother spun of its inhabitants kept her entertained for much of her childhood. The problem is the stories are real. The forest people are real, human yet not human. They are faery and beasts, thieves and angels, mutations of humans and animals over thousands of years. Then there's Dagger, a young man who distrusts the Mazikeen and Ohar, but admits to being a thief and only interested in his own pleasure. All of them want the Chameleon for their own agenda.

With the help of Ohar and Dagger, Camryn learns to control her identity so that she can walk among more than one world. Yet the more Camryn learns, the more she suspects there are too many secrets — dangerous secrets. There are no easy answers, and every decision she makes puts someone's life in danger.

Basic Blurb (94 words) – now used at all online distributor sites

Camryn Painter is a 16-year-old freak of nature. Or possibly the savior of a civilization that isn't supposed to exist. She's a human chameleon... one who transforms into the image of whoever she sees.

Escaping from a medical research facility, Camryn discovers a magical forest world. Not that she's welcome. Her new home is filled with faeries and beasts set on destroying her. Striking a tribal alliance between what she once believed were mythical beings is her only chance of survival... if she can just control her power and figure out who to trust.

Short blurb (57 words) – often used in blog posts, guest blogs or FB parties

Camryn is a 16-year-old freak of nature, an uncontrolled human chameleon. So how can she be the savior of a civilization that isn't supposed to exist? Striking a tribal alliance between what she once believed were mythical beings is her only chance of survival... if she can just control her power and figure out who to trust.

Tag line blurb (140 characters) – metadata associated with book on websites

Camryn is a 16-year-old freak of nature, an uncontrolled human chameleon. No way can she save a civilization that isn't supposed to exist.

Tweet Sample (under 100 characters to leave room for link)

*An uncontrolled human **chameleon** might be the savior of a world that isn't supposed to exist. http://bit.ly/1y3Xqe7*

Do you see hook, emotion, and payoff in each of these? Sometimes the same words do the duty of two parts of the blurb.

Consider the word choices below in each of the above examples:
  Hook – human chameleon
  Emotion – 16-year-old freak of nature, uncontrolled
  Payoff – savior of a civilization

Can you tell, even from the shorter versions what the genre is? What would be your expectations of this book if you picked it up and read the basic blurb? Would those expectations be the same for the short blurb or even the tweet?

Are my blurbs perfect? No...not by a long shot. They can always be improved. However, there is a point at which you say it is doing what it needs to do and move on to the next book.

I really did start off posting that long back-cover blurb on all vendor sites. When it wasn't working, I went back and posted the basic blurb. Results? Ten times more views, three times more sales within just three months.

How to Identify Appropriate Categories for Your Books.

Everyone thinks categories are the easiest thing to determine, when in fact they can be quite difficult. Even more important is where you choose to categorize your book also determines what the competition is and the likelihood that your book will be found among the thousands of others in that category.

Let's begin with how category selection actually works. When you load a book to any vendor site, one of the things you are required to do is to select a category that accurately reflects your book's genre. Depending on the vendor, you may get to select anywhere from two categories to five categories. The first category you select is considered the primary category.

Whenever you select a category, you want to go as deep into subcategories as fits your book. This goes back to the "big fish in a small pond" analogy. It identifies your niche audience. Let's look at the example below for a romantic suspense book. Below are three categories the author selected. The number in parentheses is the number of books in this vendor's catalog that are also listed in that category.

1. Romance > Mystery & Suspense > Suspense (68,000)
2. Romance > Romantic Suspense (17,000)
3. Teens (50,000)

First, notice that the author did not choose "Romance" alone as a category even though this book is clearly a romance. That is because the Romance category alone is at over 460,000. That is a lot of competition. You want to look for a narrow category. Don't worry if someone types in "romance" by itself. Because my narrow categories are at the root of two of the three selections, those who just type in romance have the possibility of seeing my book too.

In the first selection, **Romance > Mystery & Suspense > Suspense** the book will show up on searches of any one of those words —suspense, or mystery & suspense, or romance. It will also show up in rankings at each level of that category tree. Each level also narrows the field of competitive books. In the romance category, my book may not show up until page 50. Whereas in the narrower category my book might show up earlier.

Vendors show books based on which books the believe that reader is most likely to buy. A part of that decision is popularity. Books that are already popular are going to be shown first. New books with no track record or books with few sales are going to be shown toward the end of the listing. Wouldn't you rather be competing against 17,000 other books than 68,000, or worse 460,000? I know I would.

Let's look at one more example that would narrow this even further if it was appropriate for the book. Let's say that this romantic suspense book also had a paranormal element where the detective was psychic.

If I searched on romantic suspense paranormal, I now only have 2,900 other books to compete against. If instead of mystery & suspense > suspense I select thea category romance > paranormal > psychics I've now narrowed my competition to only 367 books! Now I'm in a really good position to compete.

What does this narrowing to do rankings and how does it help? First, if you get in the top 100 in a category—even in a narrow category—it appears on the page with your book whenever it is found. When you get in the top 100 in a category, readers say to themselves "This must be good, it's in the top 100." Even if you don't have a lot of reviews they still get this little "reader cookie" saying there must be some quality to this book. This trickles out to other categories too. If a reader found your book because of a search on your second category—romantic suspense—then when it is purchased it boosts that category ranking. In this way, ranking well in one category will also impact another category and the entire category tree.

Choosing the right category is key.

How to discover categories that relate to your book and the competition.

Let's begin with a little exercise.

1. Go to Amazon and type in the name of a book in your genre that you know well (not your own book).

2. When you get to the book page, scroll down to where it has the information about the publisher, number of pages, publication date, etc.
3. Just below that you will see overall ranking of the book (either in the Kindle Store or in Books), followed by the rankings in each category selected for that book.
4. Write down what categories were selected and how far down the tree.
5. Now repeat this same exercise at Kobo (listing in small print just below title). See if different categories were selected and if the rankings are different.

To demonstrate the "big fish small pond" syndrome on a larger scale, I'm going to share rankings (as of the date I wrote this section) on three books, each on Amazon and Kobo and all published two or more years ago. I've made a brief note about earnings comparisons next to each book title.

For a non-fiction book, DIY Publishing (I've made 5 times more money at Kobo than Amazon, though Amazon has picked up more recently.)

Amazon

- #262 in Books > Computers & Technology > Graphics & Design > Electronic Documents
- #523 in Kindle Store > Kindle eBooks > Education & Teaching > Teacher Resources > Computers & Technology
- #886 in Kindle Store > Kindle eBooks > Computers & Technology > Graphic Design

Kobo:
#63 in Nonfiction, Computers, Internet, Electronic Commerce

#18 in Nonfiction, Computers, Application Software, Desktop Publishing
#307 in Nonfiction, Computers, General Computing, Skills

Notice that the category selection at each location is slightly different. That reflects the options provided by the vendor. It would be wise for me to go back to Amazon and see if I can now choose categories closer to those at Kobo and if it will make a difference.

For my romantic women's fiction book, Undertones (Though the numbers are similar, I've made more money at Amazon because a 15K ranking at Amazon is among over a million books in the category, whereas an 18K ranking at Kobo is among perhaps 100 thousand books.)

Amazon:

- #15141 in Kindle Store > Kindle eBooks > Literature & Fiction > Women's Fiction > Romance
- #27151 in Kindle Store > Kindle eBooks > Literature & Fiction > Contemporary Fiction > Women's Fiction
- #44484 in Books > Literature & Fiction > Women's Fiction > Contemporary Women

Kobo:
#18758 in Romance, Contemporary
#48833 in Romance

Again, the category selections are different. At Amazon, Contemporary Romance is a very large and competitive category. Selecting Women's Fiction and then Romance narrows it. At Kobo, there is not an option for selecting a Women's Fiction category.

For a YA Fantasy book, Chameleon: The Awakening (Though the rankings are higher at Kobo, in this case I've made about the same money in both places. Again, Amazon competition is a larger pool of books)

Amazon:

- #6270 in Kindle Store > Kindle eBooks > Literature & Fiction > Action & Adventure > Fantasy
- #6349 in Books > Literature & Fiction > Action & Adventure > Fantasy
- #23030 in Kindle Store > Kindle eBooks > Science Fiction & Fantasy > Fantasy > Paranormal & Urban

Kobo:
#2295 in Kids, Teen, Fantasy and Magic
#2295 in Fiction - YA, Fantasy
#2295 in Kids, Fiction, Fantasy and Magic

Things to Remember About Category Selection

- Prior to uploading to a particular vendor, check what comes up in the categories you are thinking about. If the books that come up are not similar to yours that is a problem. It means that when people are looking for a particular type of book yours will not show up.
- Categories are NOT set in stone. Do the best you can. If after six months sales are awful or non-existent, try changing them and give it another six months. Do your research or describe your book to someone and ask them what they would enter in a search to find it. No fair cheating by entering the book name or the author name.
- At least once a year, go back and re-evaluate your categories. Distributors are always making changes in their selection of categories. Also, when a category is not offered, the distributor might have something in FAQs about how to get

it to come up in searches through keywords. For example, at Amazon there is no category for Young Adult fiction. However, if you use the word "young adult" or "teen" in your keywords, the book will come up in that category when that is entered in the search terms.

Final Notes: Remember that rankings vary widely from genre to genre and vendor to vendor. You cannot compare earnings and rankings for any author between stores. Certainly, if an author is in the Top 100 at any vendor it is a good place to be and provides more opportunities for discoverability and thus more opportunities for readers to purchase your book.

Sometimes the "big fish, small pond" option will drive not only purchases at that vendor but also at other distributors as word of mouth gets out to a wider audience.

In all of my examples above, I provided ebook comparisons. This is because you can't get print book comparisons as no other print book vendors provide rankings (e.g., Barnes and Noble, BAM, Book Depository, Powell's, etc.) In addition, the reality is that most authors today sell far more ebooks than print books.

This is true even in children's books, starting from about age 6 up. I am constantly amazed at the number of parents who read to their children with a tablet. I am even more amazed at the number of children who have a tablet themselves for reading.

This means if you are not distributing your book as an ebook, as well as print, you are missing out on important sales opportunities.

How to Select Effective Keywords

I'm sure you've heard that having good keywords is critical. But how do you decide what those words are? Also, how do search engines recommend books based on those key words?

Did you know that keyword searches differ from one vendor to another? It's true! At one distributor using the keyword "teen" means ages 15-21 while at another it means ages 12-16. That can make a significant difference as to if your book is found when someone searches for Young Adult fiction. In addition, users at different platforms search differently. Readers who prefer to use Barnes and Noble actually search based on different key words than users at Amazon. Yes, there are cross-overs, but you want to be sure you are hitting the most common search terms every time. Again, it goes back to knowing your audience and their "reader cookies."

The trick to selecting keywords is remembering that it's not about choosing the words *that you think* describe your book's subject. It's using the words *other people use* when searching. Keywords need to be selected carefully and placed in a hierarchy of importance. Though you can have many keywords identified in metadata on your website or blog (rule of thumb is up to 255 characters, including commas and spaces), most vendor sites limit the number of keywords or phrases you can use. Some only allow seven (Amazon), while others allow fifteen (Apple). Yet others have a character limit of 70 or 110 characters total for your keywords.

The ranked list also helps you to determine how else you will use those keywords in other media as you talk about your book. The reuse of keywords in blog posts, review sites, twitter feeds, etc. will reinforce those words and make multiple connections to your book.

Think about how you might look for a book in a search engine. If you don't know the book name or the author, but someone told you about a book they loved, what would you likely remember? A plot element? A character trait? The genre? These are the very same criteria for choosing keywords and phrases.

What NOT to Use as Keywords at Distributor Sites

Do not use any of the following information for keywords. This is because that metadata is already collected by your distributor and is already being mined and used when someone types into the vendor search engine.

Do NOT use these as keywords:

- Title
- Subtitle
- Series title
- Categories You Already Selected (e.g., romance, contemporary romance, historical, SF etc.)
- Author Name
- Character Names (if already used in the blurb)
- Dates (e.g., 1938, if already used in the blurb)
- Other author names re NOT allowed as a keyword

Things to Consider as Keywords

As always, know your reader first. Here are things that might be good to use as keywords or phrases.

Setting (WWII, urban, rural, forest, dystopian, a different planet, a specific city or country)

Character types (veteran, career woman, curmudgeon, teen, homeless, mentally ill, wizard, secret agent, femme fatale, feisty, rogue)

Career types of characters (housewife, attorney, plumber, CEO, chef, pilot, musician, engineer)

Audience (women's fiction, teen, seniors, LGBT, baby boomers, children, middle-grade, quilters, COS players)

Themes (coming of age, forgiveness, love conquers all, alienation, betrayal, revenge, survival, coming home)

Story tone (feel-good, happy, funny, scary, mysterious, satirical, dystopian, inspirational, sensual, sexy, clean)

Categories you could not select – for example Amazon does not have a YA category or a teen category. Your choice is "Juvenile Fiction" or the regular fiction categories. But you can use the words TEEN and YOUNG ADULT in your keywords.

Other keywords to consider are character names if you are writing an ongoing series (only if those character names are not already in your book blurb). Readers may look for a book based on your protagonist's name. If you write under multiple pen names and you want readers to see the cross-over, you can include your other name(s) as a keyword as well—especially if your other pen name is better known.

Tools for Finding Keywords that are Vendor Specific

It used to be that Google provided a free keyword suggestion tool with AdWords. They do still have the tool, but you have to sign in and I haven't found it to be very useful for book authors. This means the best way for you to find keywords is by going to each search engine or distributor and seeing what suggestions come up. The technique I'm going to illustrate below is with distributors such as Amazon, Kobo, Apple, or B&N. However, the same technique can be used with search engines like Google, Yahoo, Bing, etc.

Most distributors' search functions use what is termed "autocomplete" to provide customers with suggested keywords. These top keywords may change regularly, as the search engines constantly evaluate data and provide the most searched words at any particular day or hour (depending on how often it is refreshed).

In this illustration I'm going to compare the auto-complete keywords for several distributors.

I used the word "paranormal" as a start for each of them. If I have a book that has paranormal elements, but I did not select it as one of my categories, then I might want to use it as a keyword. However, I want to know if I should use it alone or in a phrase that would further delineate my audience.

In the Kobo books illustration below, paranormal brought up the following search possibilities: paranormality, paranormal media, paranormal love, paranormal state, paranormalcy (book 1), paranormal fright, etc. For Kiersten White, author of the book *Paranormalcy*, this is a great result. Her title fits the genre and is high on searches.

For myself, it makes me consider if any of these higher searches fits my books. The closest would be "paranormal love." Even though this is a young adult series, there is a love interest. So next I have to decide if I want to add that phrase in order to garner the searches of readers who specifically want to know there is a love story or love interest in the novel. The results would suggest I add "paranormal love" as a keyword to my books at Kobo.

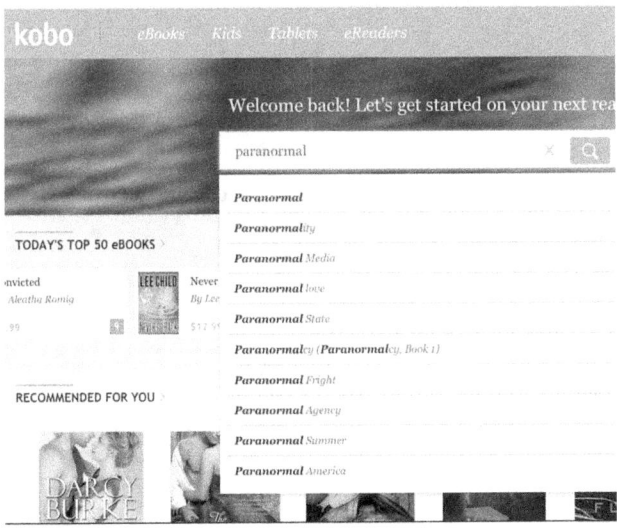

Let's try the same search at Amazon. In this case the results were quite different. As you can see in the screen capture below, "paranormal romance" and variations on it encompass five of the keyword searches. Other options are paranormal erotica, paranormal mystery, paranormal investigation, and paranormal books.

As at Kobo, "paranormalcy" is also a highly searched term which when clicked will get Kierstin White's book at the top of the page.

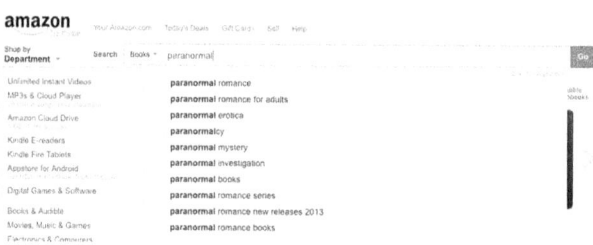

Whereas Kobo books provided insight for me to add "paranormal love" as a keyword for my book series, at Amazon I would make that keyword "paranormal romance."

Google Books and Google Play Books give slightly different results. See side-by-side comparison below. In Google Books (print) the next two options are "paranormal romance" and "paranormal activity" whereas in Google Play books (ebooks) the next options are "paranormal romance" and "paranormal pleasure."

At Barnes and Noble, the top keywords were paranormalcy, paranormal protection agency, and paranormal activity. At iTunes (Apple) the list contained paranormal witness and paranormal activity.

Tip: At Apple iTunes, searches for books are not separated from searches for movie titles. Of the major online book vendors, the information gleaned in the iTunes autocomplete function is not as useful for authors.

As you can see, keywords may need to change slightly at each vendor in order to capture the maximum number of searches. The decision I need to make if I want to use "paranormal" by itself, or "paranormal love" in order to capture that extra audience that would always put the phrase together first. When a phrase is used (e.g., paranormal love) the search engine will evaluate the words together first, and then provide results for the words separately. So you don't need to use a list of keywords that say: paranormal, paranormal love. Just as in the categories, the phrase will cover both instances.

Once a consumer enters their keyword search criteria, most distributors sequence the book displays by ranking in sales or popularity. If the keyword search is "paranormal love", then all books that meet the criteria for "paranormal love" will be displayed with the most popular or best-selling books first. Next you will see books that meet the "paranormal" criterion, again with best-selling or most popular books listed first. This might include books with no love story at all such as a paranormal thriller or a non-fiction book about paranormal activity. Finally, books that meet the "love" criteria—such as a book about a dog's love or a nonfiction book about the different types of love could follow.

One note on this display sequence. If a book has had NO sales at all it is possible that it will not show up in a search at all or will be buried so far down the list (after the ones that only meet one of the two words) that a consumer would never find it on the 300th page of the listing. For this reason it is wise to always purchase a copy of your book (or gift the book to a potential reader/reviewer) at each vendor so that the ranking mechanism is started. This is, of course, easier and less costly to do with ebooks than print books.

Again, different distributors prejudice top sellers in different ways. Barnes & Noble has options for publishers to pay for top rankings or featured books. Kobo has advertising options for pay, as well as special promo deals that anyone has an opportunity to participte in by talking to the merchandisers at Kobo—some free and some paid. Apple also has a variety of promotional options—some free and some paid. Amazon tends to be a little more egalitarian though they also have paid options. Amazon also provides certain options that are only for those books that are EXCLUSIVE to Amazon—meaning you promise not to sell the book anywhere else for a period of time.

Take a moment to select seven keywords (or phrases) for each of your books. Try them out in major search engines and at different distributors in order to see if you want to modify them based on the top search results. You will want to save this information somewhere so it is easy for you to enter it when you begin uploading books to vendors.

Sales and Almost-Sales

The #1 metric that ALL vendors use to display books is some type of sales ranking. This means that the books that are selling the most copies will always be shown first on a vendor page. There is nothing you can do to change that except to sell more copies. Depending on the vendor, FREE copies may get as much play in the rankings as paid copies.

So what if you aren't selling well yet? Or your book is just released? Another little known fact about algorithms is that all vendors also track clicks. That means people who click on the book cover to read more. Though it is not as important as a sale, it is important in terms of visibility. Once a person has clicked on a book on the site, even if the person doesn't buy, that book is saved and shown to the person over and over again. Vendors know that the customer already showed interest and there is a better chance of convincing the customer they want to buy that book than getting them to go through the random search process again.

What does that mean you should do? It means getting all your friends and fans to at least go look at the book is important. Even if they do not buy right now, just clicking on it and reading about it will give a slight boost in rankings and the vendor will continue to remind them they were looking at the book and it is still there for purchase.

Chapter Four
EBOOK DISTRIBUTION

Unlike print books where the majority of POD printing is handled by only two vendors, ebooks have a plethora of distribution options. In fact, it seems that a new vendor pops up weekly.

This chapter discusses the variety of distribution channels available to the self-published author. I will illustrate how to add accounts and upload your work at the following large distributors, and discuss the options each offers.

- Amazon
- Barnes & Noble
- Kobo
- Apple

In addition to these large distributors, there are hundreds of other possibilities. Some are genre specific such as ARe (All Romance ebooks), while others are simply e-commerce portals that purport to offer better discoverability than the large distribution options. I will also cover options that are not available for direct upload but can be accessed through aggregators—a type of middleman distributor that feeds products to larger companies (e.g., Amazon, Apple, Kobo, Sony, etc.).

In my opinion, the only reason to use a middleman for distribution is if that entity has access to markets you do not. For example, Sony only allows larger publishers to upload direct. In order to upload directly to Sony you must have a minimum of 110 titles. It is unlikely that most self-publishing authors will meet that criterion. In order to reach Sony's market, you would need to use a middleman distributor.

Other distributors also have minimums or other access restrictions. For example, Overdrive (the leading library distributor for lending ebooks) requires a minimum of five titles before you can upload direct. Apple requires that all titles be uploaded from an Apple computer. If you don't have one, you either have to find a friend who will do it for you or go through a middleman or other service to have access.

Some authors believe the percentage a middleman takes (ranging from 5-25% depending on the company) is worth it. These authors don't want to take the time to upload to each distributor or to monitor sales at each distributor. They prefer to have a person or company handle it centrally and report combined sales.

When I began self-publishing six years ago, I preferred the control I had over distribution channels. Things tended to be processed more quickly from direct loads than from a middleman company like Smashwords, and I could track where I'd made changes and where I had not. I didn't like giving up another percentage of my earnings to an aggregator.

When I only had a few books out, making changes and tracking individual uploads was no problem. However, now with over 30 titles to manage and market with frequent price pulsing and special deals, I find that my time is worth more to me than the small percentage I'm giving to an aggregator. Taking the time to upload to six or seven vendors each time and track all the stores sales and availability information was too much. Now I use Draft2Digital to manage distribution channels and reporting sales and availability. The 10% they take is significantly less expensive than my time or having an assistant do that work for me.

Note: I talk more in depth about Draft2Digital as an aggregator and why I use them in the next chapter.

You can determine what works best for you and what you are willing to pay for convenience. If you do decide to use an aggregator, make sure you know the contract terms, understand the payment schedules, and have a complete detailing of all fees and percentages the company takes from your sales.

Distribution Partners Pros and Cons

Each vendor offers different options for distributing your ebook. It is important to understand these differences, their markets, and to make informed choices. Only one vendor, Amazon, provides certain options that require the author to only use Amazon for distribution.

Finding good statistics on the market share for each of these distribution vendors is difficult. That is, in part, because it changes all the time. The appearance of a new company in the market also changes the dynamics of sales. Some newer players, like Kobo, are growing by more than 100% a year right now while others are falling faster than ever, like Barnes and Noble.

However, that doesn't mean you should write off any companies quite yet. New leadership, new vision, and new direction can turn them around. These larger companies will often buy a smaller company with good software, agility, or a vision that matches their ethos and then surge in sales once more.

Also, ebook market share statistics are reported in different ways. For example, some surveys rate ebook market share by the number of devices sold (e.g., ereaders, tablets, phones) by a vendor. In this scenario, Apple wins every time because it has sold the largest number of devices worldwide. But that doesn't necessarily mean Apple is selling the greatest number of ebooks.

Other surveys rate market share by the number of titles downloaded from a company's e-store. That makes sense, except that many companies do not offer this information in formal reporting. For example, though Amazon provides annual public reporting of its profits and losses, it does not break out ebooks as a line item to be evaluated. This means that those statistics are gathered from a limited number of resources (e.g., Commercial Publishers and Bowker), and that self-published titles that do not use an ISBN are not counted anywhere.

Other statistics are gathered from aggregators like Smashwords. This provides insight into a certain number of self-published titles, but the revenue numbers are skewed to those formats distributed via Smashwords. For example, most authors do not distribute to Amazon via Smashwords. That means that Smashwords has no data on how those authors are doing in Amazon versus the other distribution venues. Other authors only use Smashwords to distribute to Apple.

Ebook companies keep their numbers very close and report them only in press releases that interpret the data in their favor. An organization like Bowker can only report on the ebooks which have used an ISBN. This means that the Bowker report skews toward traditional publishing who uses ISBNs for both ebooks and print books all the time. However, a large percentage of indie publishers do not use ISBNs for ebooks, which means Bowker cannot gather data on them.

The Wall Street Journal reports on apps used to download books. Publisher's Weekly can only report on those ebooks that are reported to data resources primarily in commercial publishing. Amazon does not report to any of those publications, which means that numbers related to Amazon may be skewed based on "best guesses."

In other words, take the table below only as a very broad stroke of trends. Do not take the actual numbers themselves as fact. The "Others" category refers to both proprietary device collections as well as bookstores that have a large online presence for ebook sales. These are found primarily in Europe, Asia, and South America. In those regions they often make up the highest percentage of ebook distribution.

The question for the five players listed in the table below is if any of them will partner with these large regional online retailers, and by doing so change their market share dramatically. There is already evidence that both Amazon and Kobo are doing that. The extent to which these companies can build effective partnerships throughout the world will determine who, in the near term, garners the majority of the worldwide market in ebook sales.

Region	Amazon	Apple	B&N	Kobo	Google Books	Other
USA	51%	17%	13%	8%	5%	6%
Canada	25%	12%	--	52%	2%	9%
Australia	16%	22%	--	4%	15%	N/A
UK	44%	7%	6%	14%	11%	18%
Europe	29%	21%	--	12%	14%	24%
Asia	5%	27%	--	16%	12%	40%
South America	12%	16%	--	2%	41%	29%

In the table above, the Google Books downloads may represent an unusual number of free books as compared to the other four distributors.

In the following chapter, I will provide step-by-step instructions to upload your ebook to each of the four primary vendors in the chart above—Amazon, Apple, B&N, and Kobo. Google has been closed to new accounts for more than two years, so I won't provide instructions for them.

Certain requirements are common across all vendors. They all need metadata that describes the book. They all need regional pricing. You, as the author, must determine in which of the global markets your book should be sold. Each vendor offers different payments for books based on different rules. This may impact your pricing decisions. Finally, the vendors require you to upload your ebook file in a format that each of their different e-reading devices can recognize and render effectively.

The process for loading a book to each vendor is very similar. They may require a different order (e.g., load cover and interior file first, then load description data or vice versa), but the totality of information required is pretty much the same. I will go through the nuances of each vendor. If you begin with Amazon and learn that, you will have a fairly easy time of understanding any other vendor you wish to pursue.

Uploading to Amazon

Amazon is the one distribution partner that bases pricing decisions and payment percentages on exclusivity in certain markets. It is also the only vendor with a proprietary ebook file type (MOBI, also known as Mobipocket). Self-published authors and small presses upload to Amazon through their Kindle Direct Publishing (KDP) site.

Go to: http://kdp.amazon.com

If you have purchased products at Amazon you can use the same account with KDP. However, you may wish to use a different account with KDP—one that reflects your business email and address, or simply one that recognizes you by your author pen name. Don't use an Amazon that is shared with your family.

To open a new account, click on the **Sign Up** button in the upper right portion of the screen, under "Don't have an Amazon account." Follow the instructions to provide your email address, selecting a password, etc. Once you have access to the KDP section, you will be presented with a screen indicating you have no titles currently available. Click on the **Add new title** button to proceed.

The next screen will begin the process for adding a book and uploading it to Amazon. The first option is whether you wish to have this book in the KDP Select plan. You can read the details in the screen shot below. In short, it means that you will market your book only with Amazon for a minimum period of 90 days.

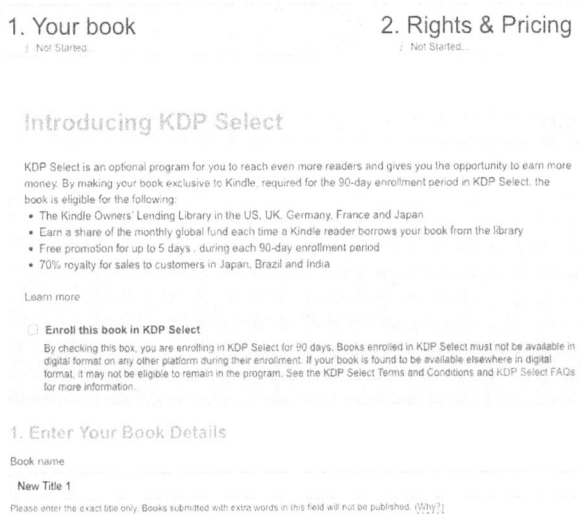

To clarify, this means you cannot sell this book anywhere else—not at B&N, Kobo, Apple, ARe, Diesel, etc. and not at your own ecommerce site or website. On your website you can list that it is available at Amazon and provide a link, but you cannot sell it independently anywhere except Amazon during this time.

I do not advocate enrolling in KDP Select. For me, the benefits do not outweigh the exclusivity requirement. I want my book to be in as many markets as possible. I also want both the ebook and print book to be available at booksellers. I have a strong commitment to supporting local booksellers.

That being said, to be fair, I will share the reasons some authors and some small commercial publishers do elect to enroll their books in KDP select. I've listed authors' reasons in rank order from the most often stated to the least.

1. Because Amazon has the largest market share in the United States, some authors wish to take advantage of that power immediately by making their book free for five days. The hope is that this will increase the books visibility online, generate reviews and buzz, and when the free period ends

the book will continue to do well because of the buzz generated from the free downloads.
2. Because Amazon has the largest market share, some authors do not plan to offer their books in any other venue. The ebook will always be offered only through Amazon. These authors believe that 50% of the market is sufficient for their sales.
3. Some authors indicate that having the revenue stream from the Kindle lending option is critical for them.
4. Only KDP Select authors can receive the 70% payment (instead of 35%) in Amazon stores in Japan, Brazil, and India.

In speaking with authors who have chosen KDP select in the past, most report that the ability to gain extensive visibility through a free book offering no longer works. This is due to changes in how free books and paid books are displayed. Numerous authors now report that where in the past they have been vaulted to top rankings by making books free, it now only works if the free offering is simultaneously paired with paid advertising during those days.

The ability to increase revenue in Japan, Brazil, and India might be a motivator if Amazon were the only ebook retailer in those countries. That is not the case and their market share is not overwhelming.

As with all things in self-publishing, each author must make her own decisions about this. If you are willing to offer your book exclusively to Amazon for three months, there is nothing wrong with trying KDP Select for yourself and testing my statements.

To put your book into KDP select, click in the area next to the box which says: **Enroll this book in KDP select**. If you do not wish to enroll, skip that box.

Complete your book details. The first step in completing your book details is to enter your book title in the field labeled **Book name**. Unlike previous programs covered in this book, there is only a single line available for your title and subtitle. If your book has a subtitle, enter it here with a colon as illustrated below. A colon in databases for print books is read as a separator to indicate a subtitle. At the end of uploading your ebook, you will want to match it to your print book on Amazon. This will help to do that.

Do *not* add anything in the title field that is not a part of your title and that does not appear on your book cover and your title page. Amazon is very strict about this. In the past some marketers would attempt to add words such as "bestselling novel" or "award winning book" or similar descriptors in the title field. Other marketers attempted to add keywords in the title field in the hopes of gaming the search engine.

Amazon will compare your title to what is presented on the title page of your submitted book. If you added extra words in your title on this page, Amazon will refuse to make the book available in its store. Leave them for the book description and keyword section provided later.

Tip: At any time during the data entry process, you can scroll to the bottom of the page and click on the **Save as Draft** button. This will save any data you've entered and allow you to come back to it at a later time or date.

1. Enter Your Book Details

Book name

DIY Publishing: A step-by-step guide to print and ebook formatting and distribution

Please enter the exact title only. Books submitted with extra words in this field will not be published. (Why?)

☐ This book is part of a series (What's this?)

Edition number (optional) (What's this?)

Publisher (optional) (What's this?)

Windtree Press

Description (What's this?)

platform for the self-published writer. However, until now, few have tackled the actual DIY steps to get your finished manuscript from your word processor, through formatting for print and various ebook reading devices, to being distributed by all the major vendors and bookstores. Lynch demystifies the technology in her easy-to-read

If your book is part of a series be sure to click in the box next to **This book is part of a series**. When clicked, an additional box opens for you to enter the series name and the book number.

Enter your series title exactly (example: The Forest People). The volume number refers to the book order in the series. If this is the first book in the series, the volume number is 1.

Completing the series information correctly is important to help readers see all of the books in a series together. Amazon will automatically display other books available in the series if this was checked and titled.

Tip: If you haven't had a series before and now you do, it helps to email Amazon support and let them know these books are all part of a series. Give them the ASIN and URL to every book in the series. They will require you to number the book order, even if they can stand on their own. This is VERY helpful in letting your readers know what other books in the series are available.

The **Edition number** needs to match what you have entered when creating your ebook file, when purchasing your ISBN, and when registering your copyright.

The **Publisher** is you or your company name. It is not Amazon. Amazon is a distributor of your book. If you don't have a separate company name for your books, then enter your name (e.g., Maggie Lynch) as the publisher.

The **Description** is what readers will see when they are browsing for your book. I advise that you use the short, marketing description here (100 words or less). Long descriptions don't display in their entirety and require readers to click an arrow to see the rest of it. You will have other opportunities to provide the longer back cover blurb description. This is also your opportunity to use more descriptive words for the book, such as "by bestselling author" or "award winning."

The next section is **Book Contributors**. This is where you indicate the author's name. Click on the **Add contributors** button. That will bring up an additional display window for your entry.

First enter the author's name as it appears on the book. If you use a middle name include that in the **First (or Given) name** field. Click on the arrows for the **Title** field to indicate the contributor's type. Select **Author**. If you have author contributors such as additional authors or an illustrator, click on the **Add another** button and go through the process again.

Once you have completed your contributors additions, click on the **Save** button to return to more information about your book. The next step is to identify the language and publication date. Notice that the language will default to English. Select the publication date from the calendar. As with CreateSpace data entry, you are not allowed to add a publication date that is in the future.

If you have purchased an ebook ISBN, enter it in the **ISBN** field. As discussed in *Secrets Every Author Should Know: Indie Publishing Basics*, it is recommended that you have an ISBN in order to take advantage of certain international markets. However, it is not required to load your book to Amazon. If you do not have one, skip this field.

Step two is to Verify Your Publishing Rights. If you wish to make your book available to the public domain—meaning it is free for others to use in their own works—then click that radio button. Most authors do NOT choose this. You should click the button next to **This is not a public domain work and I hold the necessary publishing rights**.

Step three is to Target your book to your customers. This is where you will identify the subject categories that pertain to your book. These subject categories are derived from the BISAC subject categories. Amazon allows you to select two subject categories. I recommend always selecting the maximum allowed.

To select categories, click on the **Add categories** button. This will open a screen like that below.

Narrow your category selections by scrolling through options and selecting sub-categories. First click on the general **Filter**—All, Fiction, or Nonfiction. Depending on the filter, it will then bring up the subject headings available to that top-level heading. If there is a link and plus sign (+), it means the category has lower-level headings to select. If there is not a link, then that is the limit of the category.

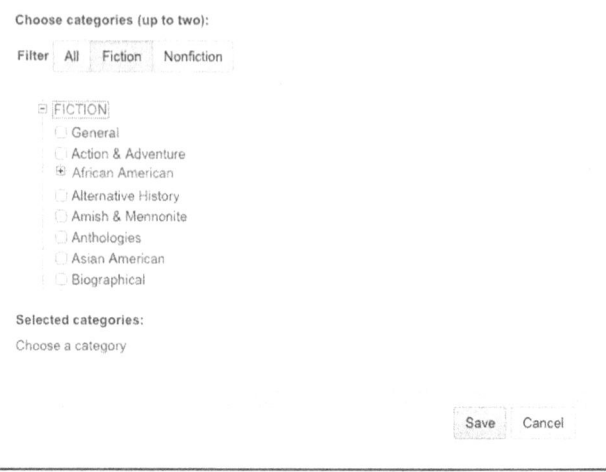

In the example above Fiction / Anthologies is the only selection. You cannot filter lower to describe the type of anthology. However, Fiction / African American has a link which will then bring up a third level of headings for selection.

Once you have identified your category, click in the box next to the heading that best describes your book. Then click the **Save** button. Your category choice will be displayed. Again click the **Add Categories** button in order to add a second choice. Repeat the process of making a selection and clicking the **Save** button.

You may come back later and change categories following this same procedure. Because you are only allowed two categories, you must delete a previous choice before making a new selection.

The next step is to type in the keywords for your book. Amazon only allows you to choose seven keywords **or phrases**. Separate each with a comma. (e.g., self-publishing, formatting, ebook publishing, etc.)

Two things are important to know about how Amazon uses metadata. First, everything you've already entered before keywords is searchable: title, author, subtitle, series title, and the subject categories. So you do not need to waste any of your keywords on those items. Second, your top keyword should be a category that was not available to you in the drop down selection previously. For example, the first keyword for this book is "self-publishing." That is the most reflective of the purpose of this book, but it was not available from the BISAC categories.

This is particularly critical in young adult fiction and non-fiction. The Amazon BISAC category selections do not have a young adult option, so young adult fiction or non-fiction is properly placed in the juvenile category. However, no one searches for young adult books using the keyword "juvenile." In my YA fantasy series, I use the keywords "young adult" and "teen" to make sure that I am capturing those searches. The remaining keywords you select should follow the advice given in *Chapter 3, Distribution Basics*.

Steps four and five are where you upload your cover image and your book file. In each case you first click on the **Browse** button to locate the file on your computer, then select it and click **Open** in your file manager. It will immediately display the file name.

Click the **Upload** button to complete the process. The cover will then display in the rectangle. The name of the book file will be displayed in step five.

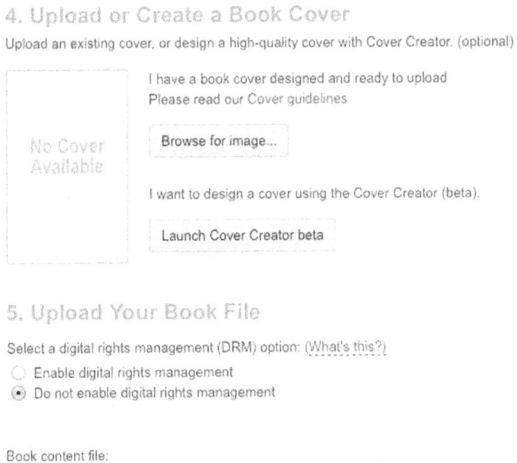

The cover image should be in JPG format. The minimum requirement is 1000 pixels on the long side. However, I recommend at least 2100 pixels in length. As phones and tablets provide much sharper image possibilities, standards will continue to rise.

As of the writing of this book, Amazon recently raised its recommendation for high definition is **2813 x 4500 pixels.** This accommodates the latest tablets (Kindle Fires) high definition screens.

I suggest you always load the larger file now and don't worry about having to come back to all your books and reload the covers in larger sizes. When I began self-publishing the minimum requirement was 600 pixels on the long side. That is no longer acceptable and many authors had to go back and reload their backlist catalog.

The reason to upload such a large image is that Amazon provides several different sizes of that image throughout its system. It can be displayed as small as 150 pixels in thumbnail in the also-bought sections or browsing hundreds of books after a search. On the dedicated book page it is usually displayed as 600 pixels tall, but users will see it larger if they go to the "look Inside" feature. In fact, users can choose to enlarge the picture, as well as text on their e-reading devices. You do not want your beautiful cover looking blurry and unreadable when it is made larger.

Amazon will accept a variety of file formats for conversion to their proprietary MOBI file type:

- Microsoft Word (.doc and .docx)
- HTML (.zip, .htm and .html)
- ePub (.epub)
- Rich Text Format (.rtf)
- Plain Text (.txt)
- Adobe PDF (.pdf)

However, providing any of these file types will likely result in a conversion where some characters or formatting is jumbled. Of the ones mentioned above, PDF is the worst. The most consistent to convert is a Microsoft Word file that does NOT have a lot of formatting.

The best way to control the look of the interior file is to upload a

MOBI file. That is the format for all Kindle devices. If you used Jutoh or Vellum or some other reliable software to create your MOBI file it will be readily accepted by KDP and should upload without issues or errors.

Once the upload is complete, you should receive feedback in green type saying "Upload Successful." If there was a problem with the uploaded contents or the conversion process, an error message will be displayed. If you are not successful at troubleshooting the problem, contact Amazon KDP support. They are very good about identifying the file and pinpointing where the problem lies.

Once the upload is a success, the next step is to preview your book in the online Kindle previewer. Though you may download a special previewer to your Kindle device. I recommend using the **Online Previewer.** It is kept up to date to reflect the latest devices Amazon offers for e-reading. It is also the way customers will view samples of your book through the "Look Inside" feature.

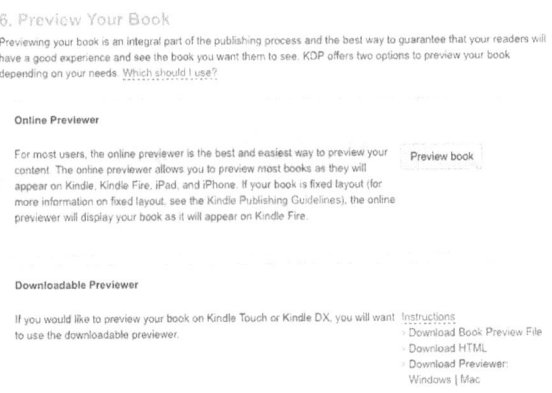

Click on the **Preview book** button and a simulation of a Kindle will display your book from the initial cover image through all of the contents. You can move through the preview by clicking the right and left arrows. Make sure that:

- the cover image is displaying on the first page

- the links in the table of contents work
- the content in a chapter accurately displays all texts, paragraphs, and headings.

The screen captures below show examples of how these elements may appear in the **Online Previewer**.

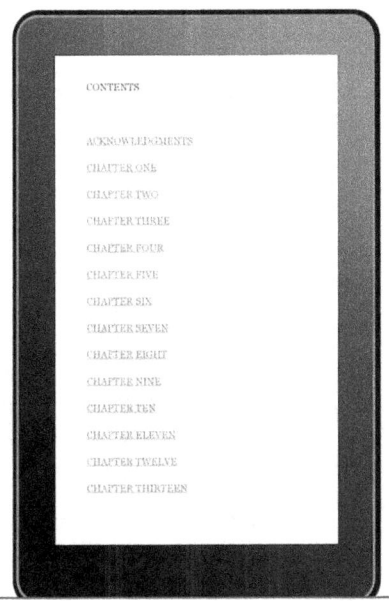

Once you are satisfied with the preview, move on to the **Verify Your Publishing Territories** section.

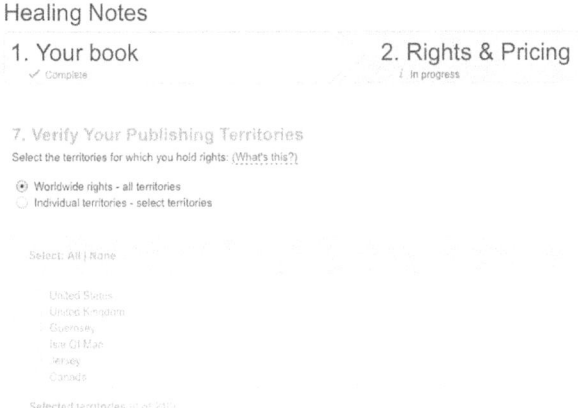

Amazon provides two options for identifying publishing territories. The first is the default, **Worldwide rights—all territories**. For most authors, this is the best one to select. It means that wherever Amazon distributes ebooks, yours will be included. When Amazon adds a new territory, your book will automatically be included there as well.

The alternative is to select **Individual territories** manually. Why would you select this? The most common reason is that you don't have worldwide rights for your work. This happens if your book was published previously by a commercial publisher and when you requested the rights back, only rights in North America were returned. Or, perhaps your publisher kept the North American rights but does not have the UK, Australia, Europe and other rights outside the U.S. and Canada.

Another reason you may wish to individually select territories is if you have granted foreign rights for your book to another publisher in a specific country. For example, after self-publishing a book in the United States, you get an offer from a publisher in Germany to translate the book into German. However, the contract also purchases the English language rights in Germany at the same time. In that situation, you cannot self-publish your book in Germany.

The next section is pricing. The payments related to your book (what Amazon calls "royalty rate") is linked to the price you set in the **Choose Your Royalty** section.

8. Choose Your Royalty

Please select a royalty option for your book. (What's this?)

○ 35% Royalty
● 70% Royalty

	List Price	Royalty Rate	Delivery Costs	Estimated Royalty
Amazon.com	$ 4.95 USD Price must be between $2.99 and $9.99.	35% (Why?) 70%	n/a $0.08	$1.73 $3.41
Amazon.in (What's this?)	☑ Set IN price automatically based on US price ₹302 ⚠ Your book must be enrolled in KDP Select in order to be eligible for 70% royalty for sales in India. Enroll now	35%	n/a	₹106
Amazon.co.uk	☑ Set UK price automatically based on US price £3.10	70%	£0.05	£2.14
Amazon.de	☑ Set DE price automatically based on US price €3.66	70%	€0.06	€2.52
Amazon.fr	☑ Set FR price automatically based on US price €3.66	70%	€0.06	€2.52

Always click the **70% Royalty** option. However, **selecting it does not guarantee you will be paid that percentage**. Amazon attempts to convince authors to price their books in the range Amazon believes is most likely to make money. In the United States, to get the maximum royalty of 70% the book must be priced between $2.99 and $9.99. Anything else receives only a 35% payment. For other countries, Amazon provides the required minimum and maximum prices to also receive the maximum royalty. I recommend staying within the maximum royalty guidelines as much as possible.

As previously mentioned, Amazon is the only book distributor that requires exclusivity for some benefits and that includes maximum royalty options. As a result of recent partnerships with other countries, Amazon now requires your book not only to meet certain pricing standards but also to be enrolled in KDP Select in order to get the 70% royalty. Currently, those countries are India, Japan, Brazil, and Mexico. All of these countries have been added in the last two years. I would not be surprised if future new country additions also follow this same requirement.

Remember: If you are in KDP Select, it means you cannot distribute your **ebook** through any other vendors outside of Amazon (not to Apple, Kobo, Barnes & Noble, etc.).

Amazon will automatically convert the price from US dollars to the currency of each country, and that conversion rate will automatically change daily as money markets change. You may choose to accept that automatic conversion or manually change it.

If you manually set the rate, it does not update to the current currency fluctuations in the market. The reasons authors choose to manually set some prices are: 1) To reflect a market norm of rounding amounts to the nearest 99 cents (e.g., $2.52 becomes $2.99); and 2) To reflect a different expectation of pricing in a particular country. In the earlier chapter on pricing, I discussed how some countries like the U.K. are showing a defined reluctance to pay more than £1.99 for an ebook. So, it may be that in that market you want to manually change the price, even if it is lower than the currency conversion would indicate.

Also be aware that Amazon deducts a "delivery charge" for each ebook sold at the 70% royalty level. The deduction is based on a calculation of the size of the book in megabytes. The typical book of about 60-70,000 words is assessed a delivery charge of about four cents. Amazon does not deduct a delivery charge on books that are sold at the 35% royalty rate.

The final decisions are to determine if you wish to participate in the **Kindle MatchBook** program and **Kindle Lending** program.

9. Kindle MatchBook
   Enroll this book in the Kindle MatchBook program. (Details)
10. Kindle Book Lending
    Allow lending for this book (Details)

By clicking Save and Publish below, I confirm that I have all rights necessary to make the content I am uploading available for marketing, distribution and sale in each territory I have indicated above, and that I am in compliance with the KDP Terms and Conditions.

<< Back to Your Bookshelf   Save and Publish   Save as Draft

The **Kindle MatchBook** program allows you to offer your ebook for free, or at a reduced rate (e.g., 99 cents or $1.99), whenever someone purchases the print edition of the same book from Amazon. A number of authors have chosen to do this in order to allow readers more freedom in how they read the same book.

Personally, I love the MatchBook program. If someone is willing to buy a print copy of my book, I want to make it easy for them to also have the ebook copy to take with them when they travel and want to finish the book. I have selected to make the ebook FREE when matched. Many other authors still opt for some payment.

I have also worked with my local bookstores to provide a similar option to them. If their customer purchases the print book, the bookstore may give them a free download code for the ebook. I think it's a nice way to continue supporting my local bookstores and providing them another way to compete with online stores.

The **Kindle Book Lending** program is required for anyone who elects to receive the 70% royalty. It allows customers to lend a book they have purchased through the Kindle Store to their friends and family. Each book may be lent once for a duration of 14 days and will not be readable by the lender during the loan period. This is similar to what people do today where they read a paperback book and then give it to a friend to read. There is no additional royalty payment for being in the lending program. The only way to opt out of the lending program is to accept a 35% royalty rate.

The final step is to click on the box next to the rights verification statement. That statement reads:

"By clicking on the Save and Publish button, I confirm that I have all rights necessary to make the content I am uploading available for marketing, distribution, and sale in each country I have indicated above and that I am in compliance with the KDP Terms and Conditions."

Complete the process by clicking the **Save and Publish** button.

It usually takes two to three hours before your book appears on the United States Amazon site. It can take up to 72 hours before it appears on all other Amazon country sites. Once it is on the site, you will receive an email saying "Congratulations! Your title has been published." That email will also provide links for you to go to Author Central and provide information about yourself for your fans.

It is highly recommended that you do follow the instructions for Author Central. At that location you can link to each of your books distributed through Amazon, link to a blog or other social media, and provide more information about yourself and how readers might contact you.

As your book is loaded on other country sites, you will get a similar email from each of those sites as well. Author Central is NOT automatically linked through all Amazon country sites. You must go to each separate country site and complete the information again.

Tip: If you do not speak the language of that country, you will want to have the U.S. site window open on one side of your screen and the country site open on the other. In that way you can match the button or input box to the U.S. translation. Also consider translating your bio through a free service like Google Translate. It won't be perfect, like a native speaker, but at least it will be understandable to those who don't speak English.

At any time that you wish to make changes to the metadata for your book, the pricing, or a new upload, your book will remain on sale with the old information until the processing is completed. This processing can take 24 to 48 hours, though it is usually only two to three hours. If your book details have not changed (e.g., pricing) after two days, contact Amazon support for assistance.

Barnes and Noble

Barnes and Noble direct ebook loads are done through Nook Press. The software at Nook Press specifically provides self-publishing authors and small presses access to Barnes and Noble distribution. Though B&N has had problems in the last few years with determining their direction, I would not count them out of the game. In fact, in some genres like Romance many authors report B&N revenues as being close to their Amazon revenues. For non-fiction, it is important that you work with Barnes and Noble. They are the largest distributor to academic institutions in the United States.

To begin the process of working with Nook Press go to: Http://nookpress.com

Click on the yellow **Get Started Now** button in the middle of the screen in order to create an account. Follow the instructions to enter your name, email, password, etc. This is a similar process at every distributor. You will be asked for your banking information at the end of the process.

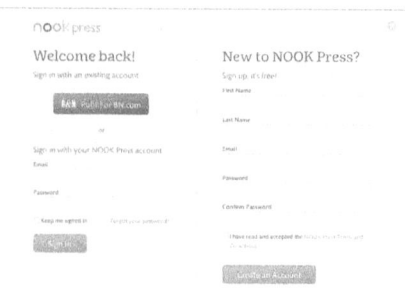

Once your account is created, an email will be sent requiring your confirmation and providing login instructions. After your login you may begin the direct load process. Unlike all other vendors, Nook Press begins by asking you to first load your manuscript before completing metadata for your book.

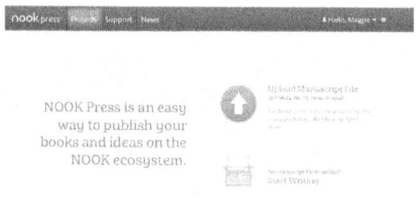

You do not have to load an EPUB file. You can load a Microsoft Word file (.doc or .docx), a text file (.txt) or an html file (.html or .htm) and it will convert that file to EPUB format. However, I strongly recommend you create your own EPUB file. The conversion engine will likely render your ebook in a way that is unexpected depending on the file type you load, how you used style sheets, and what type of linking you did.

Whether you use Jutoh, Vellum or some other means for creating an EPUB file outside of Nook Press, I recommend you do so. You will have significantly more control over the look of your ebook than allowing the Nook Press conversion engine to do it for you.

If the file upload is accepted, you will get an immediate confirmation. If there are problems with the file, you will receive an error message.

In the illustration above you may have noticed that Nook Press provides an option to write your manuscript within the Nook Press system. In addition, the platform allows authors to share their developing content with a select group of peers, get feedback, and then publish their book as an EPUB at Barnes and Noble.

I ***do not*** recommend doing this. The conversion from your online written work to EPUB is even worse than the conversion from a Word Document. The resulting file does not look at all professional. If you have a desire to write in an environment where you are sharing your work, then I suggest joining a critique group or uploading to WattPad.

Nook Press thinks of books as *projects*. You are asked to give your project a name. Then click on the **Create My Project** button to begin entering all the information about your book.

Though you don't have to use your book title, it makes sense to me that you would. It makes it easy to find and make changes later. Once a project is created, you may at any time in the data entry and uploading process click on the **Save** button at the top of the screen and exit. When you return later you may make changes and continue with the project.

The next step is to upload your cover. As with Amazon KDP, you want to upload a JPG file that is a good size. Nook recommends a minimum of 1400 pixels on the long side. I suggest you strive for the same 2100-2500 pixel size discussed earlier.

A great cover image draws customers to your NOOK Book and communicates the story at a glance. Upload your cover to make sure you get noticed!

We accept jpg, or png files between 5KB and 2MB. We recommend the height and width be at least 1400 pixels. Remember, you must have the rights to use any image that you upload.

Click on the **Choose a file to upload** button. Browse for your cover file on your computer and select **Open**. Next you will be asked if you wish to add this cover image to your manuscript.

Click on **Yes**. This will automatically make your cover display once a customer downloads the book to her Nook device. You will see a screen with your cover displayed in place of the sample blue book.

If the cover does not look right to you, you have an option to **Replace Cover Image**. This will allow you to select a different file from your computer.

Alternatively, you may choose to **Crop Original Image**. Authors will choose this if their original cover image doesn't meet the length to width aspect ratio expected. Cropping allows you to determine how to make it display optimally without having to redo your cover. Most distributors expect book covers to be created with a 1:1.5 aspect ratio. That means for every 1 inch of width, you should have 1.5" of height. This is the typical 6" x 9" trade paperback sizing.

If you are thinking in pixels, below are some typical pixel cover designs. Remember, the first number is the width. It is always advised to use the largest number of pixels to achieve the highest definition on new tablets and computers.

2813 x 4500 pixels
   1563 x 2500 pixels
   1250 x 2000 pixels (minimum)

Next you will describe your book's contents and subject categories. This data is very similar to what you put into Amazon KDP. When you place the cursor inside the first field, **Title,** Nook Press will display the fields associated with that information. Below is a screen capture of how the data was entered for this book.

```
                            Save                                        Save & Next

     NOOK Book Details - Title & Description
    * required

     * Title
       DIY Publishing

     * Publisher                          * Publication Date
       Windtree Press                       10 - October      28      2013


     * Contributors
       You may include up to five contributors.
       FIRST NAME            LAST NAME              ROLE
       Maggie                Lynch

       + Add Another Contributor
```

As in many title fields, a subtitle is not presented separately. If you have a subtitle, separate it from the main title with a colon. For example: *DIY Publishing: A step-by-step guide for print and ebook formatting and distribution* or for Fiction: *Chameleon: The Awakening.*

The **Publisher** is either you or your company name. It is *not* Nook Press or Barnes and Noble. Unlike Amazon KDP, you may select a **Publication Date** in the future on Nook Press.

The **Contributors** field works the same as everywhere else. First enter your author name, and then select the role from the drop down box as **Author**. If there are additional authors or other contributors to enter click on the **Add Another Contributor** link and define the role for that contributor.

Scroll further down the page to reveal the book description and author bio sections.

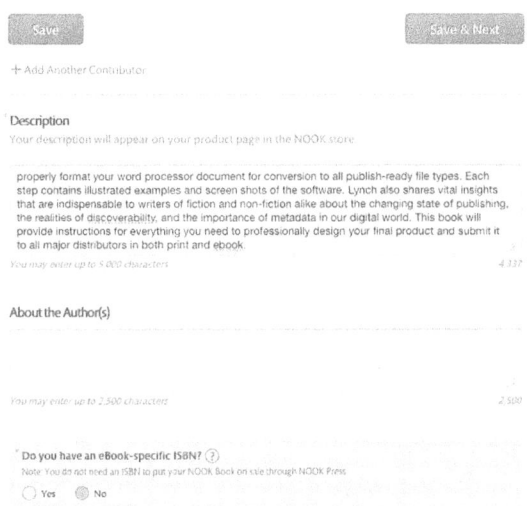

On Nook Press you are allocated up to 5,000 characters, which is approximately 500 words. However, I recommend you use the short, marketing description of your book and limit it to approximately 100 words. As discussed previously, to read the entire description the consumer will need to click a link to have it revealed. You want to capture their interest quickly so they can complete the purchase.

The **About the Author(s)** section is where the author bio is placed. Again, the short one is recommended. If there are multiple authors, such as with an anthology, be sure to include a brief bio for each author. The total character count for the author section is 2500, approximately 250 words.

Finally, you have the opportunity to enter your ebook specific ISBN. If you have purchased your own ISBN through Bowker (or are using one from a publisher) you may use that same ebook ISBN here. Select the

Yes button to see a new window to enter the ISBN-13 number for your ebook. Enter the ISBN without hyphens.

The next section is to **Add Categories**. These are the BISAC categories. As with Amazon, you click on the arrow to see the major headers available. Click on the header that best applies to your book and additional subcategories may be revealed. Select the one that fits.

Barnes and Noble allows for the largest number of category selections of any vendor. You may select up to five. Use as many as make sense to best describe the book and how users might search for it. You are not required to list five different categories.

Once you have selected the first category it will appear below the drop down box, as illustrated below. To select another category, go through the process again. First click on the down arrow and then make selections. Those subject headings will be added until you have reached the maximum of five categories.

The **Keywords for Search Engines** works similarly to what you've done before. However, instead of limiting the number of keywords or phrases, Nook Press limits the number of characters to 100, including spaces. Select keywords that are different from your category selections. A comma between each keyword or phrase separates the selections.

Finally, you are asked to identify the appropriate audience for your book and the language. Click on the drop down arrows to make the appropriate selections.

The next section contains rights and pricing. As of March 2016, Barnes and Noble distributes ebooks only in the United States. They shut down their U.K. distribution in March 2016. Therefore, this page is very straightforward.

Distribution in the United States is automatically selected.

The **DRM** section on this screen asks: Do you want DRM encryption for your NOOK book? DRM is digital rights management. This encryption restricts the buyer to downloading the book to only one device. So, if the buyer downloads to her Nook and then later decides she would rather read the book on her phone or her iPad, she is unable to move the file because it is encrypted.

Some publishers and individual authors like to use DRM because they believe it cuts down on piracy or theft. I disagree with that assessment. First, there are numerous ways to get around DRM. Instructions are easily found on the Internet. Second, ebook buyers tend to have multiple devices—smart phones, tablets, laptops, desktops, and ereaders. The device they choose to use may differ depending on their travel situation or simply wanting to change positions.

I do not put DRM on any of my books. I prefer to trust my readers to use the book for their enjoyment only. I also participate in any lending programs allowed by the distributor. So, I already know the book may be lent. DRM would exclude this option.

The **list price** is the same you use for other vendors. Enter the price in that field. It is always listed in U.S. Dollars. The royalty is automatically calculated, so you immediately know what your payment will be for each book sold at the price you listed.

The final screen before publishing is the **NOOK Book Details – Other Information** screen. This screen provides further identifying information that helps Barnes and Noble create connections between this book and any other books you may upload in the future.

The first question is: Is this Nook Book public domain? For most authors the answer is **No**. Unless you are putting it up for free and allowing others to use all or part of it, you do not wish it to be in the public domain.

SECRETS TO PRICING AND DISTRIBUTION

NOOK Book Details – Other Information

required

* Is this NOOK Book public domain?
  ○ Yes ● No

* Is this NOOK Book a part of a series?
  ● Yes ○ No
  * Series Name   * Series Number

* Is this NOOK Book available in print?
  ○ Yes ● No

The second question: Is this Nook Book a part of a series? Similar to Amazon KDP and other places you've entered book data, this will allow Barnes and Noble to create a link between this book and others in the series when they are uploaded. Type the series name exactly as it appears on the title page. The series number is the relationship of the book in the order to be read.

The final question is: Is this Nook Book available in print? If you select **Yes**, another field will pop up to allow you to enter the **Number of Pages in Print**. Barnes and Noble uses this information to give readers a sense of the length of the book. However, it does not make an attempt to display the print book and ebook together like Amazon does. Since Barnes & Noble separated the Nook platform from the print and bookstore business, it no longer displays them together.

NOOK Book Details - Other Information

*required

* Is this NOOK Book public domain? (?)
  ○ Yes   ● No

* Is this NOOK Book a part of a series?
  ○ Yes   ● No

* Is this NOOK Book available in print?
  ● Yes   ○ No

* Number of Pages in Print:
  364

When you click on the **Save & Next** button, you will have the option to **Publish.** The **Publish** button has a little shopping cart next to it. This does not mean you will be paying any fees to distribute your book. The shopping cart is a symbol to let you know you are making it available for sale on the Barnes and Noble site.

If you need to make changes to your Nook Press ebook, login to the Nook Press website. It will display the status of all the books you have uploaded. If you only wish to change the details about the book (e.g., description, price, categories, etc.). Then click on the **View Details** link next to the book you wish to modify. Your book will remain on sale, but the changes you entered will take 24-48 hours to show up on both the United States and United Kingdom Barnes and Noble sales sites.

If you wish to update the book contents or change the cover, then click on the **Update Manuscript** link next to the book. Again, the book will remain on sale with the previous version. The update will take 48 to 72 hours to replace the files on both Barnes and Noble sites.

If your book is not updated within 72 hours, contact support for assistance.

Kobo

Kobo is picking up momentum in the United States, where it is thought to have about 8% of the market, and even more so around the world. Kobo now has 16 million readers, a quadrupling of readers from 2012 when it says its sales had already doubled. Choosing not to upload to Kobo would be a mistake.

Kobo provides access to its platform through Kobo Writing Life. Go to: http://www.kobo.com/writinglife

Click on the **Sign in to Writing Life** button. This takes you to a screen where you may log in if you already have an account. If you do not have an account, click on the link that says *New? Sign up here* toward the top of the screen.

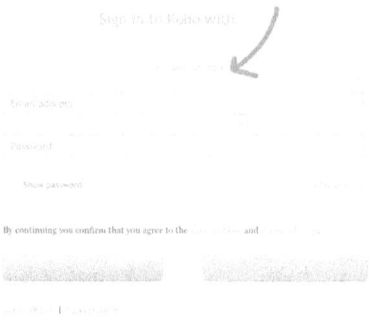

This will bring up the account creation process where you may sign up with your email address and choose a password.

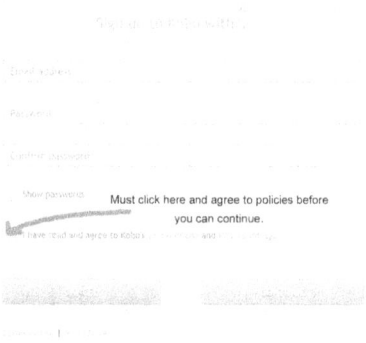

You must click in the box, illustrated with red arrow, and accept the Terms of Use and Privacy Policy. Note that these are the terms of use for every Kobo account—readers and authors. Click on the links to read about these documents. Once you have agreed to the terms, click the **Continue** button.

Next the **BECOME A KOBO AUTHOR** screen appears. This is where you will complete all of your contact information. The top half of the screen asks for the usual information. First and last name, publisher name, and email address are the required fields. In addition, you may provide a telephone number. Note that the option to receive updates, tips and information about Kobo Writing Life is automatically checked. I recommend keeping this checked. However, if you do not want to receive that information, click in the green box and you will be opted out.

BECOME A KOBO AUTHOR

CONTACT INFORMATION

First Name

Last Name

Publisher name

optional

Email address - one that we can reliably contact you at

Email updates

☑ Get email updates, tips and information about Kobo Writing Life

Telephone

Extension

optional

optional

Kobo publishing account ID

optional

If you previously had a publishing account with Kobo your account ID will help us link your old account with this new one.

There is a nice feature on this screen that may not apply to new authors with Kobo. However, it is something you may need in the future. The **Kobo publishing account ID** allows you to combine accounts at a later date. For example, if you established one account under your non-fiction writer name and another under a pseudonym for fiction, you could elect to combine the two accounts and manage all of your books and all of your sales data in one place. To my knowledge, Kobo is the only vendor that makes this so easy. All other vendors require you to request support assistance to combine accounts.

Next, scroll down to access the remaining fields in the **CONTACT**

INFORMATION section. The bottom half of the screen asks for physical location information. Click on the arrow in the **Country** field to select the country in which you live. Enter your **Street address, City,** and **Postal Code**. The **Province** drop down box contains Canadian provinces and also U.S. states. If you live in other countries with provinces or states, they are not uniquely identified in this drop down box. Selecting the country name will be sufficient for users outside of Canada and the United States.

When all fields have been completed click on the **Save and next** button. This will take you to the **Terms of Service** screen. Included in this screen are the Terms of Use and Privacy Policies you accepted earlier. The primary purpose for this screen is to make you aware of the **Content Policy**. Most vendors simply have a link to the document and a check box. However, Kobo makes it obvious what they are asking you to agree to something important by featuring this large box with links to the actual documents. You must click in the check box that reads:

I have read, understand, and agree to the Terms of Service and I am authorized to bind the author/publisher to this agreement.

SECRETS TO PRICING AND DISTRIBUTION

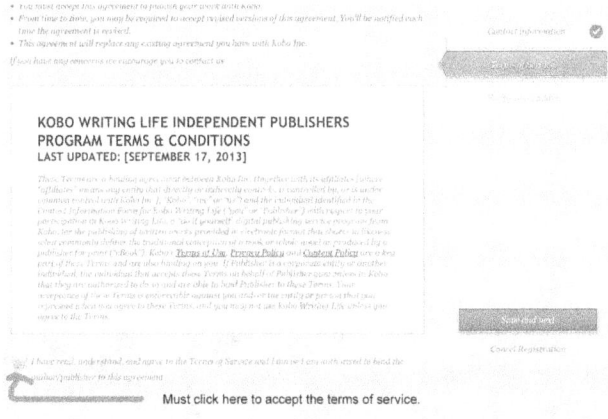

Must click here to accept the terms of service.

Once you accept the **Terms of Service**, click the **Save and next** button. This will generate an email to you that requires you to verify your email address before you may continue with your account.

After verifying your email, log back into Kobo via their instructions in the email. Now you are ready to upload your book.

Click on the **eBOOKS** link at the top of the screen. On the next screen click on the **Create New Ebook** button.

Next you will see the screen where you enter all the descriptive information about your book. It's similar to other software you've used thus far and should look familiar.

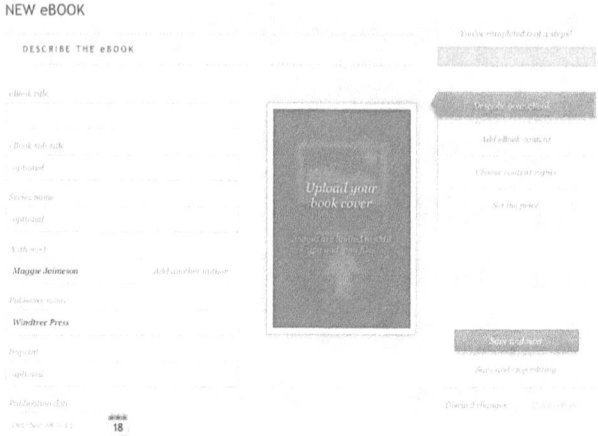

Notice that Kobo provides two separate lines for the main title, **eBook title**, and **eBook sub-title**. Whereas on Amazon you had to enter the title and subtitle together separated by a colon, at Kobo you enter them on separate lines.

Also on this screen is the **Series name** if you have one. Then type in the **Author(s) name**. To add additional authors click on the pink link *Add another author*. The **Publisher** is you or your company. Most self-published authors do not have an additional Imprint. A small press or publishing cooperative might have additional imprints.

Finally, enter the **Publication date**. As with Nook Press, you may enter a **Publication date** in the future.

Click on the book sample, where it says Upload your book cover. The image requirements are similar to other vendors. You want to upload the image in JPG or PNG. Kobo recommends that the longest side be a minimum of 2100 pixels. Again, I recommend that you upload the largest size you have to keep up with high definition devices. Once the image is uploaded the cover will appear in that space.

Scroll down to complete the book description process.

SECRETS TO PRICING AND DISTRIBUTION

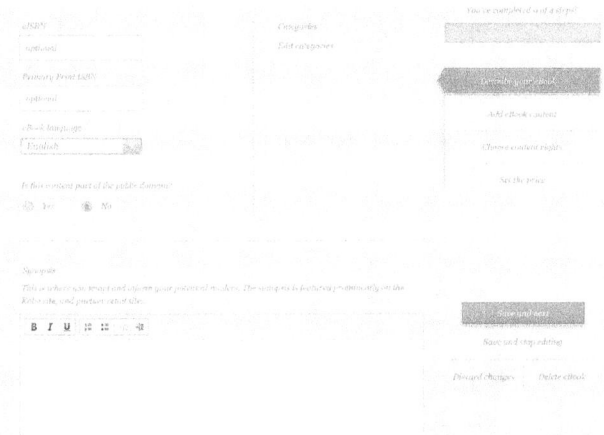

Here you will enter the ISBN associated with your ebook, the **eISBN**. If you have a print book, also enter that ISBN under **Primary Print ISBN**.

Tip: It is very important to enter the print ISBN if you have a print book. Because Kobo partners with local booksellers, this helps identify books in both formats in order for the bookseller to assist customers in their purchase. In addition, there is a rumor that at some time in the future Kobo will offer a type of "match book option" similar to what Amazon is doing.

The language defaults to English, but you may select a different language if it applies to your book.

Unless you have made the book free and available for reuse and copying select **No** in answer to the question: *Is this content part of the public domain?*

Don't miss the small pink link under **Categories**, located to the right of the eISBN field. This is where you select the BISAC categories that apply to your book. Like all other vendors, Kobo uses a drop down list with sub-categories below each arrow. It does not provide the entire BISAC list, so you must make your selections for best fit from what is provided. Kobo allows you to select up to three categories for your book.

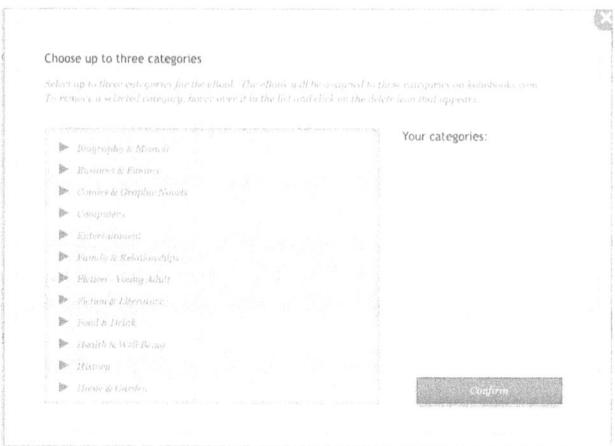

As you select each one it will appear on the screen under **Your categories**. Once you've completed your selections, click on the **Confirm** button to return to the book description main screen.

The final field on the book description screen is to enter your book blurb or back cover copy. Kobo calls this the **Synopsis.** Again, I recommended that you use the short, marketing blurb here. There is no limit to the number of characters on this screen.

Click **Save and next** to go to the ADD eBOOK CONTENT screen.

This is where you upload your file. Like other vendors, Kobo allows you to also upload a Microsoft Word (.doc or .docx) file, as well as a Kindle MOBI file or an Open Office ODT file. However, I still recommend that you upload the native Kobo ereader format, which is an EPUB file. This will provide you with the most control over the look of the content in the ereading environment.

Click on the **Upload** button to access the file on your computer. Once you have selected the correct file, click **Open** on your computer and the file will begin uploading. When the upload is complete, a confirmation of the upload will appear with a green checkmark box next to the word **Done!** It is at this point that you may download the EPUB file and preview it to make sure it is looking and working the way you anticipated.

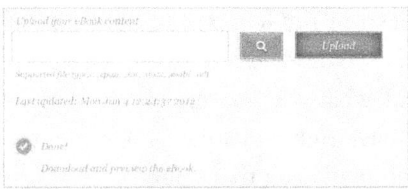

Kobo does not provide an online viewer immediately following this process. The download option assumes you either have a Kobo e-reader or have already downloaded the Kobo app to your computer.

If you do not have a Kobo e-reader, I highly recommend downloading the Kobo app for your desktop, laptop, tablet, phone, or other device to preview your Kobo ebooks. You can obtain that app at: http://www.kobo.com/apps

I use this app to preview my EPUB file prior to uploading to Kobo. If you upload an uncorrupted EPUB file, nothing will be changed in the upload process. However, if you uploaded a type of file that needed to be converted (e.g., Microsoft Word .doc file), then you will definitely want to preview the eBook using the Kobo app to ensure that the conversion engine did not add extraneous characters and that it divided the book correctly into chapters for linking.

Once you are satisfied with your upload, it is time to move to the next section, SET THE LICENSE AND GEOGRAPHIC RIGHTS.

> NEW eBOOK: DIY PUBLISHING
>
> SET THE LICENSE AND GEOGRAPHIC RIGHTS
>
> Apply Digital Rights Management?
>
> Geographic rights?
> **Worldwide rights**
> *You own the rights to sell anywhere*

The first question is: Apply Digital Rights Management? This is the DRM I discussed in the Barnes and Noble section of this chapter. Amazon applies DRM to all its ebooks. However, all other vendors give you the choice. As I stated previously, my recommendation is not to use DRM. To change the default selection click on the green box and it will change to a red box with an "X" as illustrated above.

The second question is: Geographic rights? As with other vendors, you can simply select **Worldwide rights**. That is the default selection on this screen, and what I recommend you choose unless there is a reason you do not have rights in a particular country or you know your book would have no market in that country.

As of this writing, Kobo has readers in 190 countries around the world and is adding new distribution points in these countries every month. By selecting Worldwide rights, your book will automatically be added to any new countries or booksellers in those countries where Kobo has formed a partnership. If you wish to individually select each country, click the box next to the checkmark and a listing of countries will be available for you to identify.

The final step prior to publishing your book on Kobo is to set the price. Similar to other distributors, Kobo allows you to set the price in the currency you have listed as your payments. It will then automatically calculate the price for other countries in the corresponding currency.

SECRETS TO PRICING AND DISTRIBUTION

SET THE PRICE

Pricing is complicated!
When pricing your eBook, you need to take into account your opportunities for sales in other currencies, and the royalty rates at different list price points. Find what you need to know in our user guide.

CURRENCY	LIST PRICE	OVERRIDE PRICE		ESTIMATED ROYALTY	
Your currency USD - US Dollar	4.95			70%	3.46
AUD - Australian dollar	5.52		✗	70%	3.86
CAD - Canadian dollar		4.95	✓	70%	3.46
EUR - Euro	3.72		✗	70%	2.60
GBP - British Pound	3.26		✗	70%	1.90
JPY - Japanese Yen	489		✗	70%	342
HKD - Hong Kong Dollar	38.40		✗	70%	26.88
NZD - New Zealand Dollar	6.22		✗	70%	4.35

In this illustration, my book, *Healing Notes*, is listed at 4.95 in USD – US Dollar. All author currency pricing is automatically calculated. If you wish to manually change a price, as I did for Canadian dollars, click on the box next to the red box with an x. This will change it to a green box and open a field for you to enter the price you wish to charge.

Like other vendors, Kobo also has two royalty possibilities. One is 70%, the other is 45%. For any books priced below $1.99 the royalty drops to 45%. Currently, the upper limit price has been lifted. So, anything above $1.99 will get the 70% royalty. Check Kobo's website and FAQs for updates to that royalty scheme.

Now that everything is complete, you are ready to publish the book. Click on the **Save and next** button to proceed to the final step.

At the PUBLISH eBOOK screen double-check that the publication date is accurate, and then click on the **Publish Book** button. This will put your book into the processing queue at Kobo. It typically takes 24 to 72 hours for your book to be available in the Kobo online bookstores in the United States and Canada. Once processing is complete, it is another 24 hours until your book is available in other Kobo partner stores around the world. This includes your local bookseller who is affiliated with Kobo.

You can check your book status by logging in to your Kobo account. On the DASHBOARD screen**,** click on **eBooks.** You will see a screen with books that are currently for sale and books that are Processing. To make changes to a book, click on the book cover or title link.

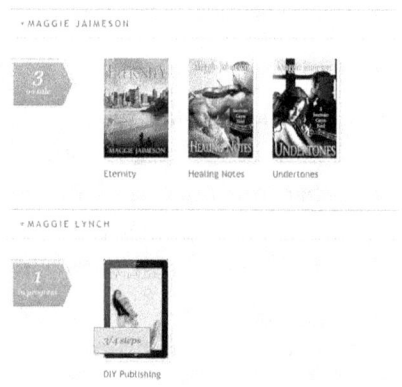

Clicking on the book you wish to review or change will take you back into the navigation structure I've covered in this section. You may change any of the data you've entered about the book and it will not have to go through processing again. However, it will take between 24 and 48 hours for the changes to be distributed to all partners around the world.

If you upload a new file (content or book cover) it will go through processing again. The previous version of your book will still be for sale. But the updated version will not be available until processing has ended—usually in 24 to 72 hours.

If your book has been stuck in processing beyond 72 hours, contact Kobo support for assistance.

Apple

Apple distribution is handled through their iTunes platform. Though you can sign up for an account via a PC, you are not allowed to physically upload files *except from an Apple device*. If you are going to use a friend or pay someone to upload your files to Apple, you will still want to have your own iTunes account in order to receive payment for your sales and manage your books.

If you already have an iTunes account (e.g., for music downloads) then you have an assigned Apple ID. If you do not have an iTunes account you will need to set one up and get an AppleID before you can sell books on Apple. My instructions assume you already have an iTunes account of some kind.

Go to: http://itunesconnect.apple.com/

Even if you already have an iTunes account for purchasing and downloading music or books, you will need to complete a separate application to distribute your content. Click on the **Get Started** link as illustrated above.

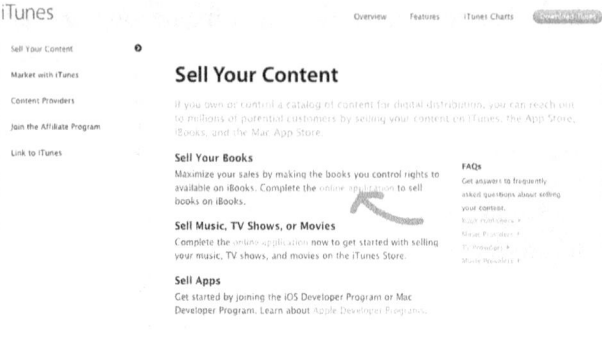

The next screen, illustrated above, provides options for selling content. Click on the **online application** link associated with **Sell Your Books**.

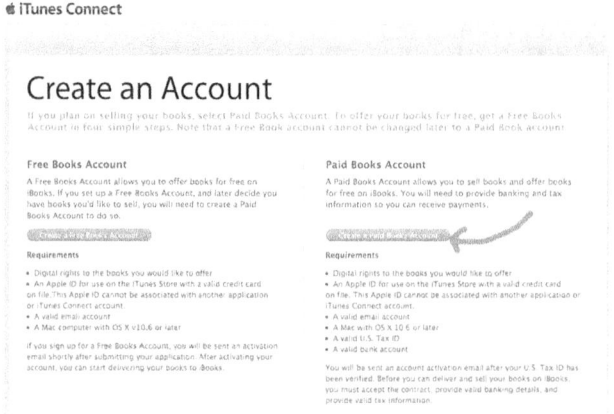

The above screen sometimes confuses people new to Apple iTunes content distribution. The choice is for a free books account or a paid books account. This does not mean that you pay a fee; it refers to whether the books you upload will be offered for free or will cost money. In the **Paid Books Account** you will be allowed to offer a book for free for short periods of time if you like. Click on the **Create Paid Books Account** button.

This will take you to the AppleID verification screen. Enter the AppleID you have already established with iTunes. You will be taken to screens to complete your bank information. It takes a day or two for Apple to verify your banking information. Once that verification process is complete, you will be provided a link to download the free iProducer application to your Apple desktop or laptop. It is then installed like all other Apple applications. You cannot download the iTunes Producer software without your being verified.

iTunes Producer is a software program that runs on your computer. It allows you to enter information about your book, attach your cover and EPUB file, determine pricing, and upload your content and cover.

Instead of doing all this online, as you have with other vendors, Apple requires you to do it within this application. The application then packages it and uploads it to the appropriate place for sale in iTunes and displays the book information on the iBookstore site. The application does NOT convert files from other formats to EPUB. Your content must already be in EPUB format.

Do not confuse iTunes Producer with the Apple iBook software. That software is designed to create fixed-format, proprietary books that will run only on the iPad. iTunes Producer accepts EPUB files and will run on any Apple device—MAC computers, laptops, iPhones, iPads.

To start entering your book information, open the iTunes Producer application. The first time you use the application you must initialize it by providing your iTunes Connect login information—AppleID and Password. The software will verify your iTunes Connect login information and then store your AppleID and password for later use when you upload your finalized package.

After initialization, each time you start iTunes Producer the application will automatically open to the package screen.

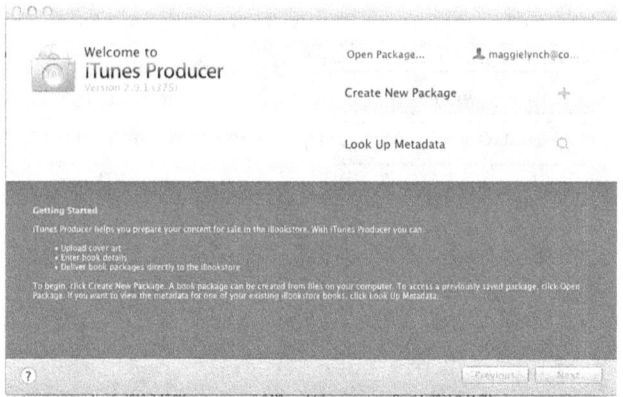

Click on the **Create New Package** button to start the book description process. During the creation process your work is saved each time you click on the **Next** button. When you come back select the **Open Package** options.

After clicking **Create New Package**, you will see a screen with the book icon selected as the default. If this is your first book upload or you are creating a new book, click **Next** to accept that you are creating a book package.

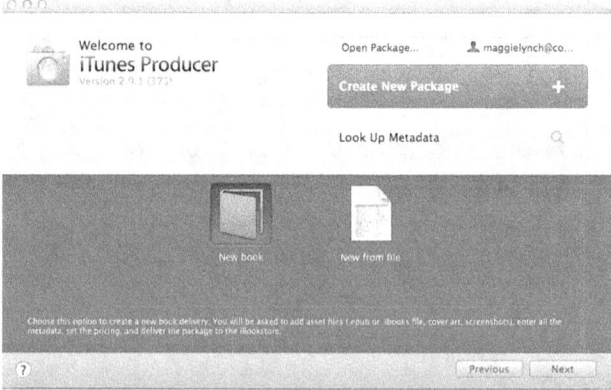

You will see a screen where you can enter the book details. This will require the same information as with other vendors.

The first field is the **ISBN** associated with the ebook. You may use the same ebook ISBN with each vendor if you purchased it yourself. Apple requires you to have an ISBN in order to upload to iTunes. The ISBN should be entered as a string of numbers, no dashes or spaces.

The **Book Type** has only two choices, Textbook or Book. Whether you are writing fiction or non-fiction, select **Book** unless you are actually preparing a textbook that would be distributed to academic institutions.

No default **Language** is selected. Click on the arrow to select the language of your book.

Note that both **Title** and **Subtitle** are available. The **Publisher** is you or your company. Similar to Barnes and Noble and Kobo, you can select a publication date in the future. The format for entering the **Publication Date** is yyyy-mm-dd. Example: 2013-10-31. Enter a **Series Name** if it is appropriate to your title and the **Number of the Book in the Series**. Skip the Store Display Number.

Enter the **Print Length**. If you do not have a print book, enter an estimate of the total page numbers based on your original manuscript file.

The **Pre-order samples allowed** box is checked by default. In order to market your book with a future publication date, iTunes automatically puts it on sale as a pre-order. This would allow the reader to sample the first 10% of the book in the same way she would if it were already available. If you do not want to allow sampling for pre-orders, click in the box to remove the checkmark.

The **Explicit Content** box must be checked for books geared to adults such as erotica, high violence, and some horror books. Be sure to check the content guidelines for Apple to ensure the book you are uploading is marked appropriately.

The **Book Description** box is where you put your book blurb. This should be the short, marketing oriented blurb. If the blurb is more than a single paragraph, you must use the HTML codes for paragraphing in order to get the spacing correct. Put a **<p>** at the beginning of the paragraph and a **</p>** at the end of the paragraph. See the example below.

<p>This book provides insights into formatting and distribution for the self-publishing author. The step-by-step ...</P>
   <p>Lynch demystifies the technology while adding information regarding the state of publishing today and ... <p>

Click **Next** to move to the subject and category selection steps. Click on **Add Category** and you will see an option to select the type of **Category Scheme** to use. The default is BISAC as that is the system used throughout the United States. However, for other countries you may wish to select BIC2 (used in the UK) or CLIL (Content and Language Integrated Learning) schemas as is appropriate for the market you are targeting. Once a category scheme is defined, the typical list of headers to click is displayed. Click on the header that best matches your book and then select the subcategory that defines the header in detail.

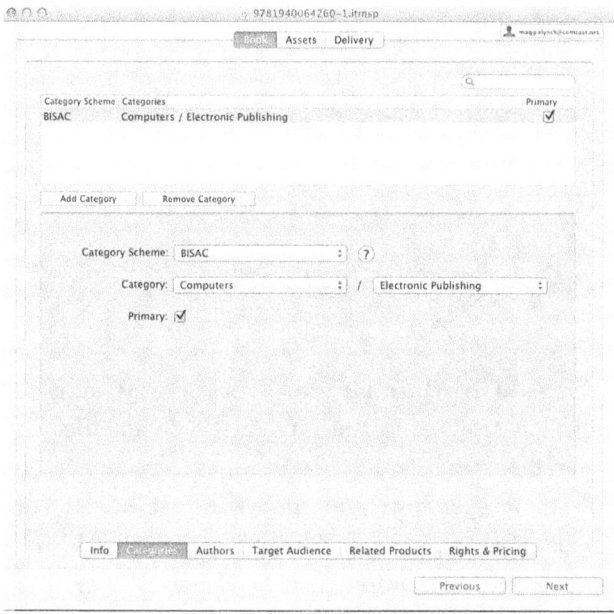

You may add up to three categories. By default, the first category you select becomes the primary category, the one you believe best defines your book. To select another category click on the Add Category button again. After selecting all of your categories, you may change the Primary category by clicking in the **Primary** box when that category is highlighted.

When you have completed selecting categories, click **Next** to go to the **Autho**r information section.

Click the **Add Author** button. Type in your author name. By default the role is selected as Author. The Sort name field lets you tell Apple to search for the name. I recommend typing the author's last name followed by a comma and then the first name. For example: Lynch, Maggie. If there is a middle name, then it would be associated with the first name. For example: Lynch, Maggie McVay.

Click **Next** to go to the **Target Audience** screen. This screen was designed primarily for textbook definition. It is not needed if the book is designed for adult readers. However, for juvenile fiction and non-fiction this screen allows you to select an age range that is most appropriate for the book. To add a target audience, click on the **Add Criteria** button.

The default is **Interest Age (in Years).** Other selections relate specifically to academic curriculum criteria. The drop down box allows you to select a specific age range for your book.

Click **Next** to continue to the **Related Products** section. This identifies other book formats that are related to the book you are uploading, such as a Print book or the same text in a different language. It does not refer to books that are related in a series.

If this applies, click on the **Add Related Product** button. The default selection is **Print Equivalent**. To make a different selection click on the down arrow.

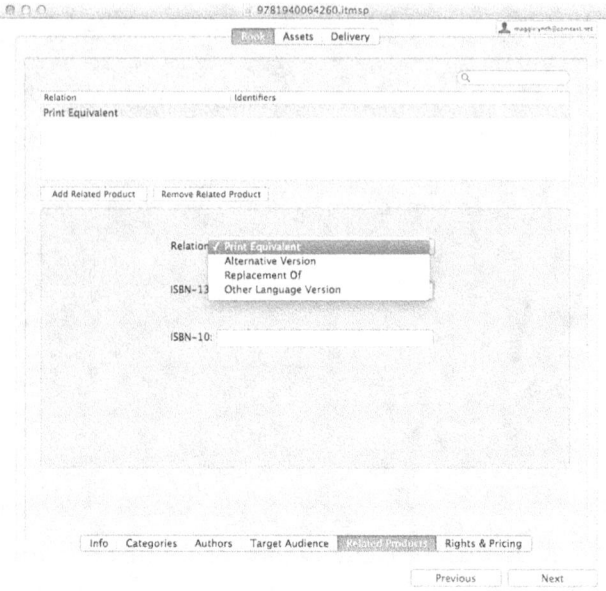

For any related book you select, you must provide its ISBN. I recommend always using the **ISBN-13** unless the book is older and only had an ISBN-10 assigned. In this section you may add as many related products as apply. Once you're finished, click on **Next** to go to **Rights and Pricing**.

Pricing works very differently in the Apple iTunes environment. First click on **Add Territory**. I suggest beginning with your own country since you already understand the currency and likely have selected a price. In the **Territory** field click the arrow to select your country. In the illustration below I selected the United States.

The **Publication Type** should be **New Release**. The Digital Only type refers only to books using enhanced features such as audio or video. This iTunes Producer software lets people upload music, so the digital only publication type also supports that.

You may elect to have a **Pre-Order Start Date** and a **Sales Start**

Date if you are timing your release and trying to build initial buzz with sales. You must upload the finished book, however, to take advantage of pre-order dates.

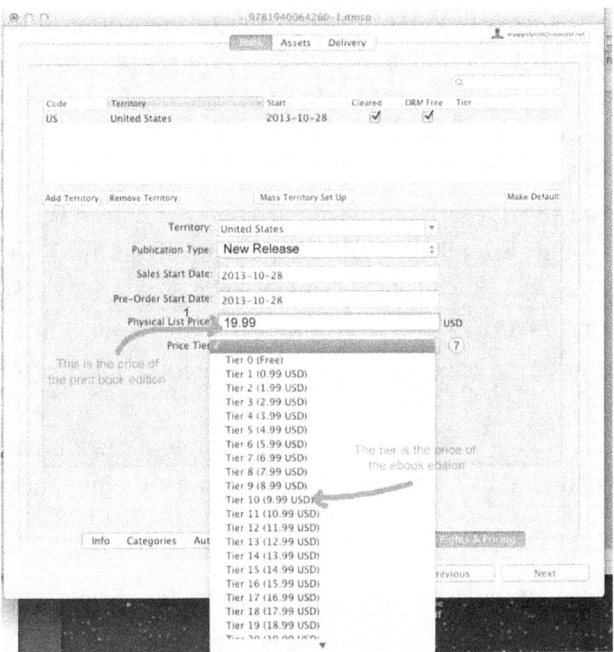

The **Physical List Price** refers to the print edition of the publication. If you have both hardcover and paperback, then use the hardcover price. Most self-published authors have POD trade paperback. Enter that print price. If the book has never had or never will have a print edition, enter what the estimated retail price would be if there were a print edition. I suggest using the following approximate prices based on word count:

- $14.00 50,000 for 60,000 words
- $15.00 61,000 for 75,000 words
- $16.00 for 76,000 to 100,000 words
- $17.00 for books over 100,000 words

The suggested pricing equivalences follow typical trade paperback pricing for fiction. If the book is non-fiction, consider raising the equivalent pricing as non-fiction expectations are for higher prices at lower word counts due to the inclusion of tables, charts, research data, indexing, etc.

The actual price for the ebook you are uploading is selected by using **Price Tiers**. The tier serves as the upper limit for what may be charged in that country for the edition of the book you are uploading. Select the price tier that matches your book. This is the price without taxes or VAT added.

To do all the countries at once, click on the **Mass Territory Set Up** button. This will take the default territory setup. In the illustration above that is the U.S. and then automatically generate pricing tiers for all the other territories where Apple distributes books. You will then have the option of selecting a different tier for a specific territory of you wish.

Once all pricing for the territories is complete, click on **Next** to go to the upload screens for your EPUB and cover files (illustrated below).

Click on the **Choose** button under **Publication**. This will open a window to your Finder (file manager). Locate the EPUB file and select it.

To offer readers a sample select the **Choose** button under the **Publication Sample** box. Most authors choose a sample that is approximately 10-20 pages. You want a sample size that is sufficient to show the writing quality and style, as well as interest the reader in purchasing the book. The sample file should also be in EPUB format.

NOTE: You only need to supply a sample IF you are doing a pre-order. If you are uploading for sale, then Apple will automatically select a 10-15 page sample for you.

SECRETS TO PRICING AND DISTRIBUTION

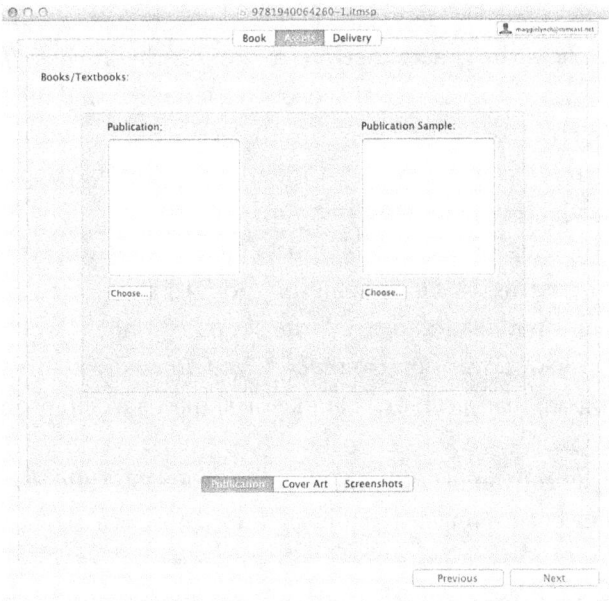

Click the **Next** button to upload your cover art. Cover art for Apple iTunes store follows guidelines that apply at other distributors. It should be in JPG format and the long side should be a minimum of 2100 pixels. Again uploading the largest file size possible is recommended.

The process for selecting the cover art is also the same as for the publication of the interior pages. Click on the **Choose** button and locate the cover art file in Finder.

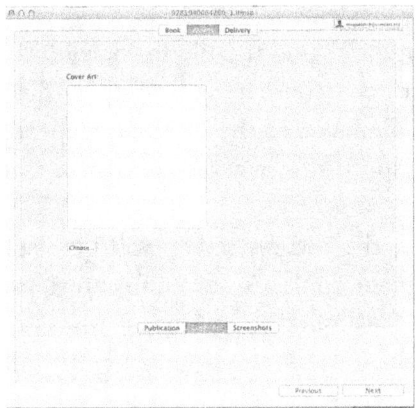

Once the cover file is selected and loaded, your cover will appear in the box. Click the **Next** button to go to the final step. iTunes Producer will try to validate the two uploaded files and all the metadata you've entered.

If everything is in the proper format, a message will appear saying: **Your package has validated correctly**.

Any problems or errors will appear on this screen. Typical problems are forgetting to fill in something on a prior screen (e.g., book description or publication date). More serious problems would be with the EPUB file or cover file. However, if you created your EPUB file in a good program like Jutoh or Vellum, you should have no problem with the validation.

Once you get the message that your package has validated, click on the **Deliver** button on the bottom right of the screen.

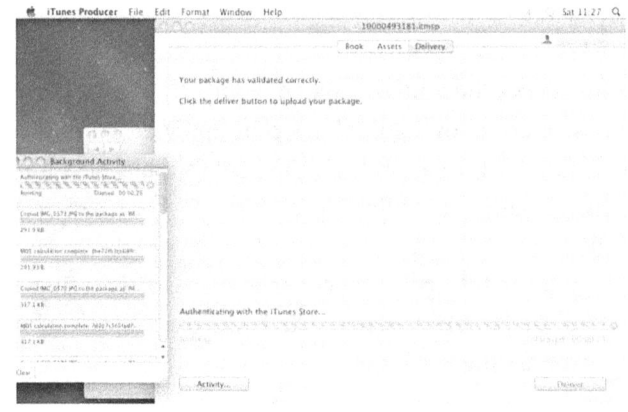

This will begin packaging the file to include all the metadata you have entered, your book content, and the cover file. It will upload the package to iTunes Connect via the Internet. Depending on the file size and your Internet speed this may take anywhere from 30 seconds to a few minutes.

If all goes well, the success screen will be displayed with a large checkmark in a green circle. A successful previous validation of the content and cover file ensure no problems.

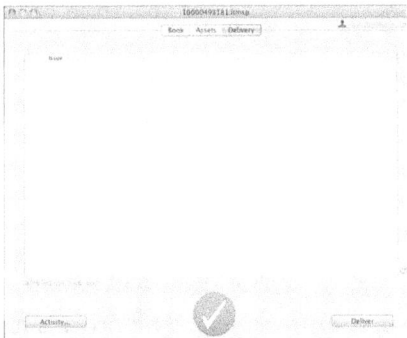

Now that the files are at iTunes, the final step is to go to your iTunes account and verify they are in your account.

Log in at: : http://itunesconnect.apple.com/ and click on

Manage Your Books.

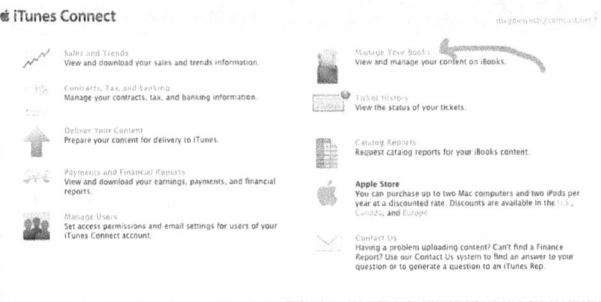

This will display all the books that you currently have loaded on iTunes and their status. In the screen capture below, notice the green dot beneath each of the books displayed. The green dot indicates the books are active and for sale in the stores.

When you first upload a title there will be a red dot. The red dot indicates the title is still processing. The processing time varies from two to five days most of the time.

Unfortunately, Apple does not notify you when the title is finally live in the iBookstore. This means you need to check back to see if it has a green dot yet. I suggest you check after 48 hours. It can sometimes take up to a week depending on time of year and the number of titles being loaded. For example, close to holidays creates a bottleneck and the processing slows significantly.

If a two weeks have passed and the title still has not gone live in the store, contact Apple support. Usually, after three weeks without proper processing, the best recourse is to delete the title from the store and upload it again.

Aggregators Can Make Distribution Faster and Easier with Only One File Upload

Many authors will recommend that you upload individually to the major vendors. The reason for this is to take advantage of any special marketing they provide for authors/companies who upload direct. However, I firmly believe in using an aggregator to cut down on the time to upload and the time to track the status and troubleshoot each platform.

For many years I uploaded direct to every platform. However, once I surpassed 12 published books, it became far too time consuming. In addition, in recent years, the promotional opportunities have now been extended to the aggregators and their customers. For example, I held off letting Draft2Digital (D2D) upload to Apple because I was afraid I wouldn't be allowed to participate in special promo opportunities. However, I finally gave in and found that: 1) My books were doing better at Apple than they had before; and 2) D2D could help me set up a promo with Apple that I couldn't get on my own previously. Myth busted!

The beauty of using an aggregator is that you load ONE file and it is then sent to all the vendors you select (e.g., B&N, Apple, Kobo, Google, ScribD, Tolino, Overdrive, etc.) Most aggregators do NOT distribute to Amazon. However, a few do. All the aggregators mentioned in this book allow you to pick and choose which ones you want them to handle for you.

The majority of authors who use aggregators choose to load to Amazon themselves, but let an aggregator load everywhere else. Some authors load to a few specific distributors themselves (e.g., Amazon, Kobo, B&N) and then let the aggregator load to the others.

There are many good aggregators to choose from. The best known and least expensive (no up front cost and take a portion of sales) are Draft2Digital, Smashwords, StreetLib and Pronoun. In addition, there are aggregators who also provide additional added cost services such as Book Baby.

It is VERY important that you know why you are using an aggregator and what channels you want them to handle for you. Carefully read each aggregators terms of service, how their commission structure is created, and how they pay. Is their cut based on gross sales or net sales and what is it? Aggregator commissions range from 5% to 20%. What have they negotiated in terms of vendor payments (70%, 50%). How often do they pay you? Monthly? Quarterly? What vendors have they partnered with and which ones do you want or need? For example, Smashwords may deliver to Baker & Taylor Blio but Draft2Digital currently does not. Street Lib has access to foreign language specific distributors that no other aggregator uses and they also deliver to Google Play.

What is most important to you? Specific distribution channels? Services the aggregator offers? Ease of using the software? Customer service reputation? Aggregator commissions from your sales? Each author has her own list of what is most important. No one aggregator is likely to meet every point on your list. For this reason, some authors actually work with more than one. They may use D2D for most distributions, but then use Smashwords to get to Baker & Taylor Blio and Street Lib to get to specialized language markets with local stores.

Smashwords was the original aggregator for indies, and I have to say Thank You to them for blazing the trail. Unfortunately, in my opinion, they haven't upgraded their software and the clunkiness of the interface, along with the requirements for loading (a 27 page document of instructions) is a deal-breaker for most new indie authors. On the other hand, Smashwords has the most channels available for distribution.

I personally prefer Draft2Digital. I have found them easy to use and they are always looking to provide value-added services for the members at no additional cost. Though they don't deliver to a couple of markets that are of interest to me, I'm okay with pursuing those in a different way.

If you are interested in some analysis around the pros and cons of these two aggregators, check out the online article by Kindlepreneur. One thing has changed since the article was written. Smashwords now also pays monthly instead of quarterly.

https://kindlepreneur.com/smashwords-vs-draft2digital/

Each aggregator has slightly different processes for loading books, getting paid, and the vendors they serve. It is up to you to determine what is the best solution for you and what you are willing to pay (in terms of percentage of sales) for that suite of services.

I will not go through the loading of books with each individual aggregator. Like the individual vendors, they all have a similar layout. However, I will go through most of the Draft2Digital load options because I am most familiar with them and they offer some things that are free to EVERYONE, not just to the people who use them to distribute their books.

I will discuss my top reasons I recommend D2D to authors. Also this article from a user new to D2D in 2016 is fairly representative of what most authors find. https://www.justpublishingadvice.com/publishing-with-draft-2-digital-a-users-review/

Who is Draft2Digital, also known as D2D?

D2D is an aggregator, similar to Smashwords, that opened in 2012. Outside of Pronoun it is the most recent arrival to the self-publishing service field and they have made a serious impact in the field for all the right reasons. There are three *strategic reasons* I use them and recommend them for long term partnership.

1. They offer things for free to authors, even if the author isn't going to use D2D for distribution. It began with providing nicely formatted ebooks from a Microsoft Word or Text document. They will convert and create files in MOBI and EPUB for ebooks and in PDF for a print book. They do this at no cost and provide the downloads for the author to take and upload wherever she wants. No one else doing this and it certainly sends a strong message of goodwill to the author community.
2. They listen to author feedback and react quickly to accommodate needs that will increase author sales, which in turn increases D2D commissions. Most software companies are loathe to change software once it's been launched. (This is a problem with Smashwords). D2D continues to be agile and strategically adds new functionality when it makes sense providing a win-win for both the author and D2D. I illustrate some of these mechanisms further below.
3. D2D keeps on top of the ebook market and takes advantage of growth areas. Again, they provide a seamless means that helps authors also take advantage of new growth areas. A recent one is their announcement to partner with Findaway Voices for audiobook distribution. This shows an

organization that is not content to rest on its initial launch and capability. That speaks to a better chance for longevity and I then want to trust my distribution to a company like this.

How D2D listens to their customers needs and reacts quickly to add automated functionality within the software.

Authors said: "I would like to write my author bio once and have it automatically appended to each ebook file." They did this. If you update your bio, they will update it in every book and resend them to all the distribution channels you've selected. This saves you from having to add it to your front or back matter every time.

Customers asked to have a way to list all their published books in the back of every ebook without having to go back and re-upload the interior content each time a new book comes out. Again D2D did this. It is all automated. It is listed by genre and series in a nicely presented sequence. You can opt in or out of using this free service. It saves me lots of time. I don't have to keep a separate list of all my books and make sure they are added at the back of every file. I also don't have to update backlist titles every time I have a new release. D2D does this automatically for me.

D2D looks at strategic sales mechanisms and provides their author customers with ways to use those mechanisms within the D2D distribution framework.

For example, D2D recognized that getting readers on a list and notifying them whenever an author has a new release would increase sales for author (and thus for D2D). So, they have a mechanism by which they append a sign-up-to-be-notified-of-releases list. Whenever the author releases a new book, D2D automatically sends a notification to the person on the list.

Could/Should the author be doing this herself? Yes, and I talk about that in the *Secrets to Effective Marketing* book. However, it never hurts to have another direct way to reach readers who may NOT ever sign up to be on your email list. Amazon does this for readers who "follow" an author's Amazon page. BookBub does this for readers who follow the author's BookBub page. GoodReads does this for readers who follow an author's GoodReads page. However, many of those readers do NOT sign up for the author's email list because they don't want to receive newsletters or other offers. All they want is to know when a new book comes out.

It is smart of D2D to provide this for authors as another mechanism to reach readers. If the author gets more sales because of this notification, then D2D also gets more in commissions.

In Fall 2015, D2D began offering a "universal book link" (UBL) mechanism to authors. This allows an author to provide a single link to their published book (e.g., the Amazon book link) and then D2D will search the Internet for approximately 20 other possible vendors that may be carrying that book. They accumulate those links and provide them all on a nice display page with attractive logos (see sample below). This allows the author to provide only ONE buy link ton their website or promo page. The other can trust that link is automatically updated whenever they add new sales channel.

Universal Book Link Display Page

On the reader side, D2D has made it easy so that when a reader chooses a particular sales channel (e.g., clicks on the Amazon logo) from the UBL page, the reader can make it the default selection. In the future, whenever that same reader clicks a buy link on the author's website or other venue the reader is automatically connected with the default sales channel making it a one-click sales experience. Brilliant!

To make the universal link even more attractive for authors to use, D2D also allows the author to list **all of her vendor affiliate account codes** so that THE AUTHOR is getting the advantage of sales made through the universal link instead of D2D getting those affiliate sales.

Even more astounding is that D2D makes this capability of universal links and affiliate codes to *any* published author, whether she uses D2D to distribute her books or not!

Why is this brilliant? First, the goodwill generated is tremendous and a good experience with D2D means an author is more likely to use them for distribution in the future. Second, though authors can list all of their affiliate accounts, the vast majority of authors don't have any affiliate accounts. And, those who do tend to only have an Amazon accounts in one country. This means for all the places an author has no affiliate accounts, D2D can use their own accounts. So, even though the service is free to authors, and authors get an easy advantage to single buy links and affiliate sales, D2D can still make decent money. A win for both sides.

D2D and Audiobook Production and Distribution

Audiobook production and distribution for indie authors has been dominated by ACX (Audiobook Creation Exchange), an Amazon company. There are other options, but the costs are prohibitively expensive for most indie authors and the process is opaque. Not only has ACX dominated the indie audiobook options, but they have also tied up distribution to Apple for a long time.

A very recent and forward-thinking offering from D2D began in July 2017. D2D recognized that audiobooks are one of the fastest growing markets for authors. So, they partnered with Findaway Voices to provide a seamless metadata transition between books already on D2D and the metadata required for distributing audiobooks. In addition, Findaway already had a good reputation in audiobook production with narrators, quality control, file packaging, and had at least a decade of identifying hundreds of audiobook sales channels around the world. ACX provides only three sales channels: Audible; iTunes; and Amazon.

Does D2D get a cut for sending authors in that direction? I don't know, but I suspect they do and I don't begrudge them that cut. It's just another example of how they keep up with the market and adapt their software to give an advantage to authors that may not otherwise be easy for them to access. I talk a lot more about Findaway Voices and the marketing opportunities they provide in the book *Secrets to Effective Marketing*.

D2D Distribution Channels (as of August 2017)

- iBooks
- Barnes & Noble
- Kobo (including Kobo Plus)
- Overdrive (serves thousands of libraries worldwide)
- Inktera (formally Page Foundry)
- Scribd
- 24Symbols
- Tolino
- Playster

On their list to add in the near future are:

- Ingram
- Google Play
- Amazon

D2D currently does not distribute to Amazon or Google Play (only Street Lib and Pronoun do that). For me, I will probably always distribute to Amazon directly. It is an easy process and I don't need a middleman for that. I could change my mind if D2D offers some assistance on foreign sites distribution, or some integration with Author Central. Given how proprietary Amazon is, I doubt that will happen.

Because I am already on Google Play books, I do not need distribution there either. I am also very concerned with how Google books does automatic discounting which impacts Amazon pricing. The one-file-for-all-channels option for D2D doesn't play well with Google's current operation. So, unless D2D extracts a promise from Google NOT to discount books (which some big publishers have negotiated that option), I won't be using them for Google.

Because D2Ds customer service value is to make it seamless to not only move books to each channel for distribution, but to also provide insider advantage to promotional opportunities, it takes good negotiation and software testing prior to them opening a new channel. There is further expansion on the horizon and I'm fine with waiting to see what additional distribution opportunities they provide.

Here's a nice YouTube video tutorial on how to upload to D2D: https://youtu.be/wl1MpWorXn8?list=PLtx8SWu1fa0qvL6rNLxo4aRK5H5XHeFnA

Two Cool Advanced Options Even Regular D2D Authors May not Know About

Check out the "Advanced User Options" tab on your **My Account page**.

A Public Sales Page—Under advanced options, you'll find the option to add a sales page that includes the book's cover and description, as well as a link that sends readers to everywhere that book is sold online. These make a great product page for your book, which you can easily link to from your website or social media posts! And they're retailer agnostic—meaning they'll work regardless of where your readers prefer to buy their books. *Note:* This is the same page as the Universal Book Links page discussed earlier.

Submission to Goodreads & Other Catalog Sites—A lot of readers check Goodreads and other catalog sites to see how a book does with other readers, and to add the book to their reading lists. Adding your book to these catalog sites manually can be a pain. That's why letting D2D do this makes it easy.

Under the Advanced User Options on the My Account page, you just select "**Submit Books to Catalog Sites.**" Every book you distribute through D2D will automatically be submitted to Goodreads and other catalogs similar to that.

Direct Ebook Distribution to Independent Booksellers

In addition to the Kobo partnership with booksellers around the world, there is another way to interest independent bookstores in selling your ebooks. That is through the use of download cards. The music industry has been using these cards for over ten years. Now, the same capabilities are being provided to authors.

A download card resembles a credit card. The front contains the book cover art. The back side contains a unique, one-time-use download code and instructions. If you order 250 cards, you receive 250 unique download codes. Companies that produce these cards provide the digital media hosting and a custom website landing page for the book and card. These companies do not take a percentage of the sale. The money is made in the upfront charge for the card manufacturing and fulfillment. Though prices vary from one company to another, they typically run between $1.50 and $3.00 per card depending on the number of cards ordered, their size, and the type of material used in the manufacturing (e.g., plastic, heavy card stock, etc.).

Download cards can be sold by bookstores with whatever specific discount you negotiate. I give a 30% discount of the ebook retail price. This is similar to the discount most distributors require (Amazon, Kobo, Barnes and Noble, etc.) to sell my ebooks at their online store. I am also experimenting in one bookstore with packaging a free download card if the customer purchases the print book. This is like a "match book" program that brick and mortar booksellers can use with their customers.

The illustration above shows the front and back of the download card I have for my DIY Publishing book. (the access code is only a sample) These cards are sold through bookstores where I have a relationship. The size of the card is 2.125" x 3.375" and the codes expire in two years.

Each vendor has different sizing options and policies regarding code expiration dates.

You may use these download cards in any way you like. You can give them away as prizes, sell them at signings where you are managing the purchases yourself, or sell them on your website. Use them in whatever way your creative marketing suggests.

Though there are many companies offering these cards, the three below are ones that have been recommended to me by people I trust.

Drop Cards http://www.dropcards.com
   Greenerside Digital http://www.greenersidedigital.com/
   Enthrill http://www.enthrill.com/endpaper/author-cards

When evaluating a potential download card provider, consider asking the following questions:

- How will they handle the different file types you want to distribute (PDF, EPUB, and MOBI)? Will customers have an option to select the file that they want, or will all three files be distributed with each download?
- Does each card have a unique one-time, secure download code? You do not want all the cards to have the same code.
- Does the system allow you to gather email addresses from customers? Can it be an opt-in to your mailing list.
- What type of reporting do they provide and how do you access it?
- Is there a time limit on how long a card is active? Also, if there is a charge to increase the time limit if needed? This is important if you buy a large number of cards, but may take a year or more to sell them all.

Of the three recommended companies above, turn around time for manufacturing and delivery of the download card varies from two to four weeks depending on the company. Drop Cards is able to do rush orders with a three to five day turn around, but you do pay Fed Ex special shipping fees for that.

Chapter Five
PRINT BOOK DISTRIBUTION

This chapter discusses the two primary distributors of the print-on-demand (POD) books that most self-published authors and small presses use. Even large publishers, like Avon, with ebook first subsidiaries (Avon Impulse) use POD books for print distribution.

The POD printing technology is primarily owned and operated by two large companies: Ingram, through its Lightning Source subsidiary (known as Ingram Spark to most indie authors); and Amazon, through its CreateSpace subsidiary. I will discuss the pros and cons of working with each company, and illustrate how to add accounts and upload your work at each vendor.

In addition to these two large print distributors, there are hundreds of other "author services" companies which will format your print book, create a cover, and arrange for POD printing and distribution. There are significant fees associated with these services, and some will additionally take a percentage of each sale.

Because ALL of these author services companies use either Lightning Source or CreateSpace for printing, I highly recommend that you upload directly to them yourself. You will receive the maximum royalty and control over how your titles are loaded and what data is associated with them.

Let's begin by comparing CreateSpace and Ingram Spark (the Lightning Source subsidiary where indies upload their books for print). Both are reputable companies that produce library-quality books using a print-on-demand model (i.e., books are printed and shipped to fulfill customer orders). While some services overlap, each company has its strengths and weaknesses. Your preference depends largely on your needs and objectives.

In my opinion, the end product is equal between these two POD vendors. In fact, CreateSpace often uses Lighting Source's POD printers when volume overwhelms its own network; and they primarily use Lightning Source printers for their expanded distribution outside the United States. In spite of those facts, there are fans on both sides that will shout from the rooftops that their POD printer is better.

The reality is that both companies have times when printers breakdown, employees don't do their best work, and a package is shipped that has problems. A single problem package does not define a company. Simply contact them, explain the problem, and both companies will ship you a new print job at no cost.

The table below shows some of the differences between the two POD companies. The prices are based the following typical fiction book configuration:

300 page (~ 75,000 word) book, perfect bound paperback binding, cream paper and a matte finish for a color cover. Retail sale price for book set at $12.99

Costs	CreateSpace	Ingram Spark
Book Setup	$0	$49*
Changes	$0	$25
Catalog Entry	$0	$12 (annually)**
B&W Interior	$4.45	$4.83
Color Interior	$21.85	$8.40
Profit if sold on Amazon	$3.32 *** -$14.20	$1.02 *** - $2.55
Profit if sold elsewhere	$0.72 *** -$16.80	$1.02 *** - $2.55
Wholesale Discount	60% Expanded 40% in Amazon	You select from 20% to 55%. Norm is 55%
Format allowed	PDF	PDF
Ease of file setup	Easy	Hard
Pay Frequency	60 days after sale	90 days after sale
Customer Service	Email, Phone, usually responds within 2-3 days. No fees ever to solve a problem.	Email only, usually responds within 1 week, tends to offer to "fix it" with a fee associated. $25 is the norm.

*Book setup fees are often waived based on sale pricing during the year, membership in an indie writer organization like Alliance for Independent (ALLi), or because you are moving a large number of books (10+) from CreateSpace to Ingram.

**Ingram charges a fee for being placed in the Books in Print catalog that is distributed to libraries and bookstores. You may opt out of this. Like the other setup fees, there are ways to get out of this fee as well during sales pricing and belonging to certain organizations.

***Profit calculated based on setting the wholesale price at Ingram at 55%. This allows for maximum discount of 40% to booksellers and libraries which is the expected discount. You may elect to set a lower percentage for wholesale but it is NOT recommended.

The profit on top is for the book with a B&W interior. The profit on the bottom is negative for the color interior. Neither Ingram Spark or CreateSpace would allow you to create a POD book where you owe them money with every book printed.

For the book specified here with the color interior, you would be required to raise the retail price to at least $15.55 to make a one cent profit through Ingram Spark. The cost for a color interior at CreateSpace is so much more than Ingram, that the book price would be astronomical. I would not suggest you even try a color interior book through CreateSpace.

Note: The vast majority of fiction books are B&W interiors. Some non-fiction books, particularly those with photographs or illustrations may need color. It is important for the author to evaluate whether the addition of color versus B&W is necessary given the added cost.

Want to do your own calculations based on your book setup? You can go to the calculators through the links below.

Calculator Links:
   Ingram:

https://myaccount.ingramspark.com/Portal/Tools/PubCompCalculator

Createspace:
https://www.createspace.com/Products/Book/Royalties.jsp

Weighing the Pros and Cons

There is a lot to take into consideration when determining whether to use Ingram Spark or CreateSpace. For the new author CreateSpace is definitely easier to use, and the user interface is fairly friendly.

However, once you begin planning print books strategically and expanding your horizons to worldwide print options, Ingram Spark definitely offers better distribution access. But it comes at a cost. That cost is an assumption that you know what you are doing in creating a print book and won't need much technical help. Or you are willing/able to pay for technical help up front (e.g., a book interior designer).

Let's look at some of the differences between the two platforms and how it applies to your potential distribution needs.

Discounts to Booksellers. The CreateSpace wholesale discount is higher than Ingram Spark at 60% versus 55%. Though Ingram Spark allows the author to choose a discount less than 55% it doesn't pay to do that. Most booksellers will not stock your book NOR order your book with a discount less than 40%. The pricing difference between CreateSpace and Ingram Spark is the difference in each vendor's cut of the sale.

However, be aware that you will have to raise your book price (through Expanded option in CreateSpace) in order to sell that book on Amazon outside the U.S. and on any other bookseller sites (e.g., B&N, Powell's, Rakutan, U.K. bookstores like Waterstones or Foyles, etc.) Do you want two different book prices for the same print book?

The Ingram Spark cut is 15% before the book goes to anyone else.

All other booksellers, including Amazon, expect a minimum of 40% discount to stock your book. This allows the bookseller to play with sales pricing and still make a profit.

So, the 40% discount to Amazon or any other bookseller makes the total discount 55%. If you try to offer less than 40% to Amazon, they will list your book as out-of-stock and available in six weeks. This kills any chance of a print book sale at Amazon. In addition, other bookstores will not stock your title because the discount is too low. They MAY order it as a special order if requested.

If you want your book to be priced the same for everyone then it may pay to go with Ingram Spark.

Tip: *Another alternative is to price the book the same everywhere but use Createspace for Amazon book sales (larger profit to you) and Ingram Spark for book sales everywhere else.*

Why use Ingram Spark to distribute to Amazon?

In the above section on discounts, you can see that using CreateSpace to distribute to Amazon provides the highest profit margin. So, why would you want to use Ingram Spark to distribute to Amazon?

There is only one benefit that only Ingram can provide if you use them to distribute to Amazon instead of CreateSpace. Ingram allows you to do print book pre-orders on Amazon. Even though CreateSpace is an Amazon company it does not allow you to do print book pre-orders.

Note: *I suspect this will be remedied in some future iteration of CreateSpace or KDP print-on-demand offering.*

Is the ability to do print book pre-orders enough to use Ingram instead of CreateSpace for Amazon distribution? Not for me, but my print sales are not stellar so doing pre-orders in print are not on my radar. On the other hand, if I could count on a thousand or more print books in pre-order, it would definitely be worthwhile.

Who is Best to Use to Distribute to Booksellers Outside of Amazon?

Again, it depends on your goals. If you have aspirations to distribute your print books worldwide, and to libraries, you may prefer Ingram Spark. However, if you want to focus on the American bookseller market then CreateSpace may be an option.

Here are the basic pros and cons of distribution outside of Amazon with each platform.

Advantages of CreateSpace

- No set-up fee for each book.
- No annual fee to be in a catalog.
- Printing and shipping costs in the U.S. are lower than Ingram Spark.
- Customer service is markedly better than Ingram Spark.

Advantages of IngramSpark

- Distribution through Ingram opens markets to virtually all bookstores and libraries throughout the world.
- Ingram offers hardcover books (CS does not).
- More trim size options are available through Ingram (physical size of book) than CreateSpace.

Both CreateSpace and Ingram distribute to OnDemand Books. This is the company that provides content to Espresso Book Machines installed in some larger Bookstores, Libraries, and Universities around the world. A customer pays for the book, and then it is printed immediately (takes about 5-6 minutes) on the local machine. Some bookstores that have these machines currently include Barnes & Noble, Powell's, American Book Centers in Netherlands and The Hague, most large university bookstores around the world, and large libraries around the world.

You can check for installations here: http://ondemandbooks.com/ebm_locations_list.php

Still Confused?

If you are just starting out, have a very limited budget, and technology is not your thing, then definitely go with CreateSpace and use the Expanded option to distribute outside of Amazon.

When you want to expand your print book options to libraries or universities, or to focus on particular international markets then it is time to look at Ingram Spark. At that point you should be making more money and you will have built a network of people to help you with the technical aspects of producing a good professional print file that can be uploaded to Ingram Spark without problems and extra fees.

The reality is that there are far too many books for booksellers—even large ones—to carry all the books customers want. The chance of any bookstore stocking your book are small, even for many bestselling authors. So, focus on ebook sales and use print books as a counter balance to pricing and for those few readers who will only read a print book and are willing to pay for it.

What do I Do?

For the past 5 years I've used only CreateSpace because the frustration for using Ingram was more than I was willing to take on. I didn't want to learn or pay for InDesign—Ingram's suggested software for the best book interior design, and I didn't want to pay for a book designer for my print book interiors.

However, I did some experimenting with one book two years ago regarding sales with Ingram distribution and sales with CreateSpace distribution. The Ingram distribution doubled by print book sales. Now, that's not a lot because I didn't have that many print book sales in a year (maybe 100-150 on average for any one book). But doubling to 300 caught my eye and made me reconsider.

Fortuitously, Vellum—a Mac only Software for formatting ebooks now has an upgrade for also formatting print books for both CreateSpace and Ingram Spark. It produces beautiful books through a series of template options. I loaded my first print book to Ingram Spark a few months ago and it was accepted without a problem!

I am in the process of moving all my print books to Ingram Spark for distribution everywhere except Amazon. This opens up potential purchasing by libraries, universities, and a variety of bookstores.

I will continue to use CreateSpace for distribution to Amazon stores and for ordering small numbers of my own print copies. Shipping from CreateSpace is less expensive AND faster in quantities under 50 books. My usual orders for special events are 10-20 books.

However, larger quantity orders (50 books or more) are less expensive from Ingram.

Loading Books to CreateSpace for Print Book Distribution

The types of data and information you are required to provide to CreateSpace will be similar to the requirements for for loading your ebooks to various vendors.

To begin working with CreateSpace go to:
http://createspace.com

You will have to set up an account before you can do anything with your book. The account set up process is similar to everywhere else on the Internet.

In the drop down box for "What type of media are you considering publishing?" select **Book**. Then click on the **Create My Account** button.

CreateSpace offers you two ways to navigate through the upload process. One is to go one step at a time; the other is to present all the requirements on a single page. Either way you will see exactly the same options to complete. I will break the selections into different sections and spend time on each.

The first screen asks for **Title Information**. Like many other online software programs, the required entries are labeled with a red asterisk. However, the more information you provide, the more metadata will be generated for your title and passed on to all distributors.

SECRETS TO PRICING AND DISTRIBUTION

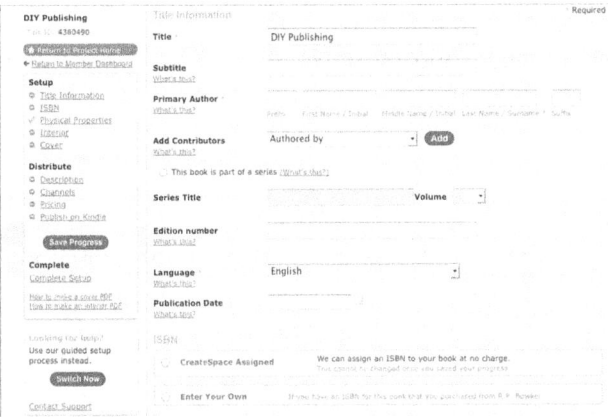

Note that this screen allows you to enter both your **Title** and your **Subtitle** on separate lines. Be sure that the title listed on the **Title** line is exactly the same as it is in your ISBN purchase and Copyright Registration. Any discrepancy in the title may result in errors when the book is released for sale.

In the **Primary Author** field, enter the name exactly as it appears on the book. Do not use a prefix unless it also appears on the book. For example, do not select Dr. Martha Jones if the prefix "Dr." is not a part of the author name. The same applies to suffixes like Jr.

Options for adding more than one author or other types of contributors are available in the **Add Contributors** section. With each contributor added, select the role of that contributor in the drop down box. Then click the **Add** button. The contributor is not added until the **Add** button is clicked.

If your book is part of a series, click in the check box next to **This book is part of a series**. That will unlock the **Series Title** and **Volume** fields. Enter the series name exactly. The volume refers to the book number in the series.

Enter the appropriate **Edition Number** of your book. If this is the first time the book is published, you don't need to enter anything as it is the first edition.

The language will default to **English** unless you change it. The publication date is the month, day, and year the book will go on sale. You may click on the calendar to select the date or enter it in the format of MM-DD-YYYY. You will not be allowed to select a date in the future.

The next section is where you will enter the ISBN. As stated earlier, an ISBN is required for every print book. If you elect to take the Create-Space ISBN, click in the radio button next to **CreateSpace Assigned**. Otherwise, click the radio button next to **Enter Your Own**. A pop up screen will open to allow entry of your ISBN.

Always enter the thirteen-digit ISBN, even though you are presented with an option of ISBN-10. Today, all bookstore online systems use the **ISBN-13** for tracking and integration with Ingram.

The **Imprint Name** is the publisher. That is you or your company. This must be the same name used when you purchased the ISBN—your name or your author name or your publishing company name.

Note: When you have your own ISBN, CreateSpace is never the imprint. The only time CreateSpace becomes the publisher or imprint is when you use the CreateSpace ISBN. Think of CreateSpace as the printer for your book.

Prior to distributing your book, CreateSpace will run a check of your ISBN against the records at Bowker and other ISBN agencies around the world. If both the book title and imprint name does not match, it will generate an error. You will not be allowed to distribute the book until the error is resolved.

Now that the title information is complete, you can move on to the sections that describe the physical properties of the book, including the trim size (height and width), the type of paper you wish to use, and whether the interior will be printed in full color.

As discussed in previous sections, most authors do NOT require a full color interior. This is very costly to print. If your book is a graphic novel, consider the difference in costs between black and white renditions of your panels and color. Will your readers be willing to pay the hefty surcharge for color books?

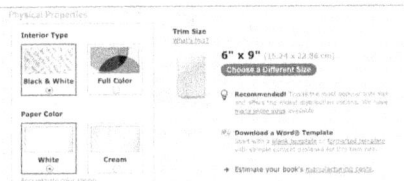

CreateSpace offers a multitude of trim sizes. The two most popular for POD books are 6" x 9" and 5.5" x 8.5". Unit costs are based on the number of printed pages, not the size of the book. Larger books require fewer pages and therefore cost less.

CreateSpace also offers a table that provides the maximum page count allowed for each trim size depending on interior color and paper color. See that at the link below:

https://www.createspace.com/Special/Pop/book_trimsizes-pagecount.html

I personally prefer the 6" x 9" size. It feels substantial and keeps the cost down. However, a book under 50,000 words may also seem too slim to a consumer. In this case you may wish to select a smaller trim size or to use a larger font to create more pages.

The next decision is whether to print the interior in **Black & White** or **Full Color**. Printing in color is significantly more expensive. There is not an option to print only certain interior pages in color and the rest in black and white. Most narrative non-fiction book and novels are printed in black and white. Children's picture books, photography books, and other genres that contain numerous images should be printed in color.

The final choice in this section is the paper color. Choose **White** or **Cream**. Some would argue that, traditionally, genre fiction is printed in white and literary fiction is printed in cream. I don't agree with that. I've looked at a lot of New York books and haven't seen that distinction. However, I would say there is a leaning toward cream in general.

Personally, I prefer white because it has higher contrast and is easier to read. The paper is also slightly thicker. There is a slight difference in cost, but it is only pennies. I recommend selecting what matches your aesthetic.

Once the physical properties section is completed, move on to the **Interior** section. This is where you will have the opportunity to upload the PDF file containing the content of the book. Earlier in this book, I described how to use a template and save the completed manuscript as a PDF file. It is that file that you will upload here. Click on the **Browse** button to locate the file on your computer. Then click **Open**. It will place the file name and location on your computer in the field next to **PDF Interior File**.

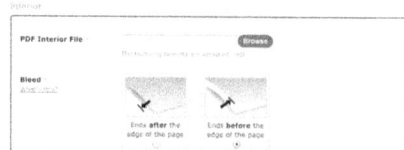

The **Bleed** refers to how much of the printed page will go into the margins. On the majority of books, you would choose the option showing a white margin around the edge. It is labeled **Ends before the edge of the page**.

The only time you would choose the left option, **Ends after the edge of the page,** is if there is an illustration or photograph that takes up the entire page and you want no white space around it. Again, this might be selected in a photography book or an art book or heavily illustrated children's book.

The bleed gives the printer a small amount of space to account for movement of the paper and design inconsistencies. It is very difficult to print exactly to the edge of a sheet of paper. In order to achieve this, printers use slightly larger sheets of paper and then trim the entire book to the required finished size. For example, a finished book with a 6" x 9" trim, uses 6-1/8" x 9-1/8" paper. Images, background images and fills that are intended to extend to the edge of the page are created to extended beyond the trim line to give a bleed. CreateSpace provides templates with bleed lines for those who need to fill an entire page with color.

The next section provides options for uploading a cover. Though CreateSpace allows you to create a cover using a standard template online, I don't recommend it as it provides a generic cover. As I emphasized earlier, the cover is the number one marketing tool for an unknown author. It is the first thing a reader sees. Therefore having a well-designed cover is critical.

A part of that cover design process is understanding bleed and creating a cover that wraps the front, spine, and back of the book. CreateSpace has a nice template generator that will provide the exact dimensions needed for the cover and bleed based on the page count, trim size, and interior design selections. You can find that template generator here:

https://www.createspace.com/Help/Book/Artwork.do

Do not guess on the page numbers. Put the exact number of pages in your PDF file. This includes front matter and all back matter. The spine calculation changes based on the number of pages. A discrepancy of as few as 25 pages can make the difference between the spine fitting securely or being loose.

Once you have the cover PDF ready to go, click on the radio button next to **PDF Cover File,** and select **Browse** to locate the file on your computer.

The next section is called **Distribute**. However, it is really descriptive information about the book and you. This information becomes a part of the metadata shared with all sales entities. Assuming you are going to elect to be distributed by Ingram and Baker & Taylor, it is this next section that will appear in the online catalogs beside the book, will categorize the book for search engines, and will provide the author biography.

The first box, labeled **Description**, is for your book description. Again, remember this description is what will appear next to your book. I recommend you use the short 100 word description—the one that is geared for the quick browsing reader and is marketing oriented. If you choose, instead, to use your back cover blurb here be aware of the 4,000 character limit which is approximately 400 words.

The next box is the **BISAC Category** selection. CreateSpace does not provide all the BISAC categories here. For both fiction and non-fiction, remember to select the lowest level sub-category that pertains to your book. In that way, your book can be searched in that category and each of the levels leading to that sub-category. For fiction, the category head is "fiction." Select a subcategory following that. You also have the option to enter the BISAC code instead of using the category selection tool. To do this click on **Enter a BISAC code**. I would choose this option if the categories presented in the scroll are not sufficient to describe the book accurately.

Remember: You can find the full list of BISAC subject headers and codes at: http://www.bisg.org/what-we-do-0-136-bisac-subject-headings-list-major-subjects.php Click on the subject header that fits your book and then find the best category description. The BISAC code is next to each line of description.

For example, when I scrolled down the list to classify this book, the closest option was Computers / digital media / general. That didn't quite fit. It said nothing about publishing or ebooks and I doubted readers would search "digital media" to find a book on self-publishing. I went to the BISAC listing at the website above and found a category for Computers / electronic publishing. That was much more accurate. Then I selected **Enter a BISAC code**, and entered the COM065000 from the list. This now provides an accurate categorization for my book and I know that it will be easier for readers to find.

The final part of describing the book is contained in the **Additional Information** section. Here is where you will provide your author biography and keywords in addition to other data.

To include your author biography, click on the **Add** button. This will open a window for you to copy and paste your biography. As I advised in the book description section above, I also recommend this biography be under 100 words if possible. Remember, this is to market yourself and your author brand.

```
Additional Information (optional)
Author Biography        Add
What's this?
Book Language           English
What's this?
Country of Publication  Choose one
What's this?
Search Keywords
What's this?
Contains Adult Content
What's this?
Large Print
What's this?
```

The **Book Language** will default to English. To change that, click on the arrows and select the appropriate language.

The **Country of Publication** is where the book originates, not where it is sold. This will be used to match the ISBN digits referring to country of publication.

The **Search Keywords** are critical. This is the opportunity for you to provide additional categorization details that you were not able to provide in the single BISAC code selection. CreateSpace limits you to only five keywords or phrases, so select carefully. Because of the five-keyword limit, do not use any of the words already provided in the BISAC categories. For this book I choose: self-publishing, formatting, distribution, style sheets, cover design. None of these words were in the BISAC category description of computer or electronic publishing. Remember to separate your five selections by commas.

The next button is labeled **Contains Adult Content**. This relates to more than sex or violence. It takes some judgment on your part. CreateSpace describes this selection as: "*If the content you provide for* *your product's detail page is not suitable for minors under the age of 18, your product may be suppressed from some search, browse, and merchandising results to protect customers from inappropriate content.* CreateSpace also states: "*No modifications will be made to your product's detail page.*"

Given ongoing media scrutiny of ebooks in general, and self-published titles in particular, I recommend evaluating your book content carefully when making this decision. Follow this link to learn about the CreateSpace content guidelines.
https://www.createspace.com/Help/Rights/ContentGuidelines.jsp

The final option is to designate if this book is a **Large Print** edition. Large Print is defined as a font size of at least 16 points. Most self-published authors do not provide a large print edition. If you are doing so, definitely click on this radio button. It will allow your book to be included in a special list for sight-impaired readers.

With the availability of ereaders, many sight-impaired individuals have chosen to take advantage of the ability to enlarge print at any time. However, some readers still appreciate a paper copy with large print.

You have now completed the descriptive portions of your book. The next step is to determine pricing and in what markets you would like your book distributed. CreateSpace offers three markets at no cost. The include distribution through the CreateSpace online store; through Amazon U.S.; and through Amazon Europe. The Amazon Europe option includes all countries in Europe where Amazon distributes. I recommend you opt to take advantage of *all* of these markets.

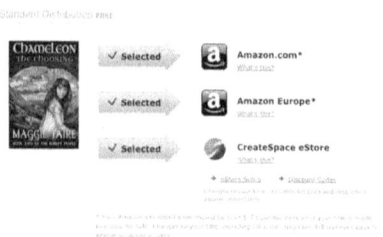

To select a market, click on the green arrow marked **Select** associated with each option. It will confirm your choice by changing color from a green to a blue arrow and marking it as **Selected** as illustrated above.

The next decision is **Expanded Distribution**. CreateSpace no longer charges for this service. This again provides three options: CreateSpace Direct sales; library sales; and bookstores and online retailers. The library sales option is only available to you if you use the CreateSpace assigned ISBN. Later, I will talk about how you can get library sales without using this distribution channel at CreateSpace. Let's evaluate each of these distribution channels.

CreateSpace Direct is the wholesale pricing option that is supposed to simulate what a commercial publisher might offer. However, I do not give much credence to the value of this channel. Many self-published authors report they have received no sales from CreateSpace Direct. Bookstores will not order direct from CreateSpace because the discount is only 20% and that is too low to be profitable. In addition, the majority of bookstores refuse to order from an Amazon subsidiary.

What makes **Expanded Distribution** worthwhile is the "Bookstores and Online Retailers" channel. This is the option that provides distribution through Ingram. It provides you access to over 28,000 bookstores around the world. Your book will be available in their online catalogs at large stores such as Barnes & Noble, Books A Million, and WH Smith, as well as at your small local bookstore. There are also a number of large online retailers for print books such as The Book Depository; Abe Books; and Powell's Books which feature the Ingram catalog.

Choosing expanded distribution does NOT guarantee your book will actually be stocked in any of these stores. Nor does it guarantee your book will actually be purchased by any library. All it does is make your book available through the purchasing network that bookstores and libraries use.

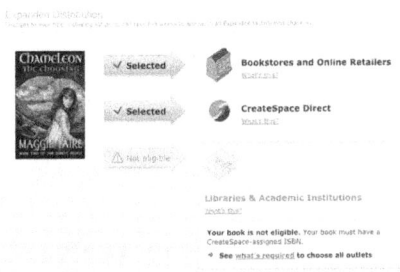

The third channel is distribution to library and academic institutions. CreateSpace restricts access to this option only to those who have elected to use a CreateSpace-assigned ISBN. I don't believe it is worth taking the CreateSpace ISBN to have this channel available. There are three other ways to get access to library distribution. First, if you register your copyright (detailed in *Chapter 14*), your book is added to the *Books in Print* publication and data feeds that are distributed from the Copyright Office to libraries and bookstores across the United States. Second, most libraries order books either from Baker & Taylor or Ingram. Under the Expanded Distribution channel you are already distributed by Ingram. Third, if you are a publisher with at least ten books you can work directly with Baker & Taylor or Ingram to enhance sales options to libraries. (Note: This costs money, usually paid through an annual contract for services.) There are also other options for free and paid services available.

Once your distribution channels have been selected, the final step is to determine the price you wish to set for your book.

Pricing Trade Paperback Books

In CreateSpace, the **Pricing** screen is presented with the cost of your book already calculated based on the number of pages you uploaded and the information you provided earlier about paper type and trim size.

Beneath each distribution channel, a minimum price is also stated. This is the price CreateSpace indicates is required in order to participate in that channel. That minimum price is based on your cost for the book, plus the discount offered to the vendor. You cannot have negative (red numbers) profit!

For example, the discount at CreateSpace Direct is only 20%, so the minimum price for any book distributed by CreateSpace is only 20% above your cost of the book. If your book cost is $4.00, that means your book most be priced above $4.80. The minimum list price is displayed next to each channel.

On the other hand, the discount to Amazon is 40%. This means the price must be higher to distribute there. Finally, the discount to Expanded Distribution is 60%.

Authors often mistakenly believe this means their local bookseller receives a 60% discount on books. That is not the case. The 60% discount is distributed so that CreateSpace keeps their 20%. That means a 40% discount is offered to wholesalers Ingram and Baker & Taylor. (The same percentage Amazon is taking) The wholesalers then take 15% to manage their distribution process. That means the discount passed to the local bookseller is now only 25%. Is it any wonder they don't regularly stock their shelves with self-published or small publishers' POD books?

List Price			Channel	Royalty
$ 14.00	USD*	Calculate	Amazon.com	$4.87
Minimum list price for this title is **$8.83**		What's this?	CreateSpace eStore	$7.67
			Expanded Distribution	$2.07
☐ Yes, suggest a GBP price based on U.S. price		What's this?		
£ 9.20	GBP**	Calculate	Amazon Europe For books printed in Great Britain	£2.58
Minimum list price for this title is **£4.90**				
☐ Yes, suggest a EUR price based on U.S. price		What's this?		
€ 10.75	EUR**	Calculate	Amazon Europe For books printed in continental Europe	€3.17
Minimum list price for this title is **€5.47**				

What CreateSpace lists as **Royalty** is the money you will receive in that market for each book you sell. In the illustration above, for one of my books, you can see that with a list price of $14.00 I will make the most money from the CreateSpace eStore at $7.67 and the least money from Expanded Distribution at $2.07.

Realistically, I will never make the $7.67 per book because *no one* buys from the CreateSpace estore except me. Readers don't buy from the store, even when I provide the link. Booksellers don't buy from the store because their discount is only 20%.

So what about purchases at the Amazon stores? In my personal experience, very few people buy print books from the Amazon stores. In 2012, with four titles available I sold a total of 17 print books at Amazon stores. So that $4.87 cent per book and its equivalents in the U.K. and Europe only materialized for 17 print books. In expanded distribution, at the $2.07 per book royalty I sold another 148 print books. Though still not a lot of money, it means of the royalty amounts I'm most likely to sell books in expanded distribution. That is the pricing determinant for my books. You cannot set a different list price for each distribution type. You must select one list price.

For me, 70% of my print sales come from my direct relationships with bookstores, which I will discuss at the end of this chapter. Those relationships and discounts are outside of CreateSpace and their distribution partners.

Looking at the choice I made above, many authors have asked why I chose to make over $2.00 per book in expanded distribution? Am I just greedy? Shouldn't I price the book as low as possible in order to get more readers? I could have priced it at $11.99 and made six cents per copy. If the price was decreased by $2.00, would it have made a difference? The answer is no.

Unfortunately, POD book pricing from Ingram and Baker & Taylor at the 25% discount to bookstores is insufficient for them to make a profit. Most bookstores' overhead (employee pay, building rent and maintenance, etc.) is about 25% if the store is running lean. That means once a store pays for shipping, it loses on the sale. The only way a store doesn't pay for shipping is to order a minimum of 15 copies of a book.

Unless your book has already proven to be popular that is unlikely to happen. This is why local booksellers don't stock self-published POD books and why they don't order your book through their normal channels. Some stores will order it for a customer who makes a request. Others will not, unless it is priced high enough that after shipping there is at least a 10% margin.

Selling Direct to Bookstores

As I said earlier, 70% of my print sales come from my relationships with bookstores. Because of that I definitely believe it is worthwhile to undertake direct print distribution. This means I purchase books from CreateSpace at my cost and then deliver them to booksellers based on their orders. I do this in two ways. For local bookstores, I keep an inventory of my books at my house. I then deliver them in batches of four or five as their stock depletes and they order more. For bookstores that are not local, I again purchase the books from CreateSpace at my cost. Then I drop ship them to the bookseller. Depending on volume, the bookseller may pay for shipping.

This scenario requires two elements: a bookseller discount of at least 40%; and a relationship built on proof that your books can sell and that you can be counted on to deliver on time. The discount is the minimum I've found that is acceptable to booksellers and allows them to make a profit. The relationships are built one store at a time. Once you have five or six stores working with you, it expands more quickly. Booksellers belong to organizations. They talk among themselves about authors they like, and authors they don't. If you've been a part of helping a bookstore succeed it will get passed to others and then those stores will contact you.

Working one-on-one with booksellers also means we can plan special events together. I can partner with them on sales and promotion. The more I do to help them, the more they do to help me. It is a win-win scenario.

There is a downside to this arrangement. The more stores you supply, the more time consuming order fulfillment, event planning, and promotion becomes. Also, this is not something you can do when you feel like it. Nor is it something you can put off because you are on deadline to get the next book out and will be hiding in your writing cave for a month. Booksellers expect to receive a book within three days of ordering. This means you need to be on top of orders and fulfillment every day, not once a week or once a month.

By this time, it would be natural to wonder why bother with print books at all. For me there are several reasons.

1. Some readers prefer print and being able to satisfy them is important to me.
2. Many reviewers, bloggers, librarians, and bookstores take you more seriously if you have a print edition available.
3. When the print book is listed on Amazon, the cost of the ebook next to it looks like a great bargain. My $4.95 ebook is a good deal next to the $14.00 print book.
4. If you enjoy book signings, you need a book to sign.
5. If a book takes off, your print need will go up. If you reach bestseller status, both booksellers and librarians will be purchasing books in high enough numbers to get free shipping and realize some profit—even on POD.

Finally, I admit I love having a print book to hold in my hand. Though I read ebooks almost exclusively, I do pay for print books on occasion. What is more special than your own book? I also frequently gift a print book to relatives, friends, and to my loyal readers through contests.

One final comment on pricing. It is important to first erase the comparison of trade paperback to mass market. They are not the same product nor are the printing costs the same. Mass market is printed in lots beginning at about 10,000 units. That is how the price is kept low. Trade Paperback for most independent writers is printed on demand, one at a time.

Instead compare your price to book to New York trade paperback books. The list price for most trade paperbacks falls between $13.95 and $17.95. Do not look at the sale price on Amazon. Compare the list prices. Should you charge the same price as a bestseller? Probably not; you don't have the following. Aim for a couple dollars under trade paperback book pricing in your genre. Charge enough to make at least $2.00 per book.

Pricing low is making a statement about how you value your work. You are saying that your book is not as good as those from New York. If you believe that, then your book is not ready to be sold. If you know your book is ready and it is comparable to the average traditionally published book, then don't price low out of fear. Price based on value —a comparable value to other trade paperback books in your genre.

Is it okay to make less than $2.00 per book. Sure. There are some authors that believe it is more important to try to get their books stocked than to make any money. They believe by pricing to make only 25 cents per print book is fine. I don't agree with this, because I don't believe bookstores choose to stock products based on price. They choose stock print books based on one thing only—do their patrons want the book. Popularity and patrons asking for it are the primary considerations.

Finally, determine what your expectations are for your print book. If all you want is something to show your family and friends, and perhaps take to a bookstore signing, then don't do expanded distribution at all. This means your print book will only be available through Amazon. However, you can still purchase your own books through CreateSpace and take them to book signings on a consignment basis. For many authors this is enough.

Personally, I like options for worldwide distribution. I don't like limiting my print distribution to one vendor. I also adore bookstores and want to support them as much as possible. But those are my choices. Do what is right for you, your goals and values, your career plan, and your economic philosophy.

Loading Books to Ingram Spark

As I said before the Ingram load process is similar to CreateSpace. The primary difference is in the loading of your cover and interior files.

The first step is to set up your account at Ingram Spark. Go to: http://ingramspark.com and complete the process for setting up an account. Similar to all the other accounts you have set up at other vendors (e.g., CreateSpace, Amazon, Kobo, etc.) it will require your name, address, phone, social security or business tax identification number, how you want to be paid, etc. Once all of that is completed you may begin loading books to Ingram Spark.

Everything begins with your Dashboard. This is where you may look at books you've already loaded as well as start a new book. The process I will illustrate here is loading your first book.

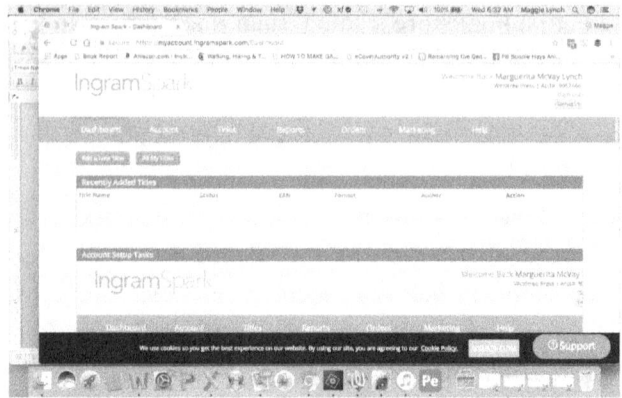

Add new title by clicking the button in the top left below the Dashboard tab that says: **Add a New Title**

The next screen will provide you with several title options: print, ebook, or print and ebook. My advice is to select only print unless you want Ingram to also to all distribution for your ebook as well (an additional $25 set up fee). I personally prefer to use D2D for aggregator distribution and load my own ebooks to Amazon. However, there are a few authors who like the one step process of using Ingram for everything.

The first screen requires you to input the book title, subtitle, short description (350 characters or less), and long description (your full book blurb). Once you have completed those elements click the yellow button at the bottom that says: **Continue to Step 2**.

Each subsequent entry page will provide an opportunity to move backward or forward as you complete the book loading process.

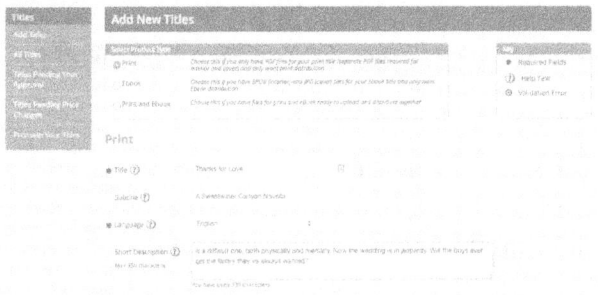

Add Title Descriptive Information

The next step is to add the author, or other contributor information as illustrated in the screenshot below.

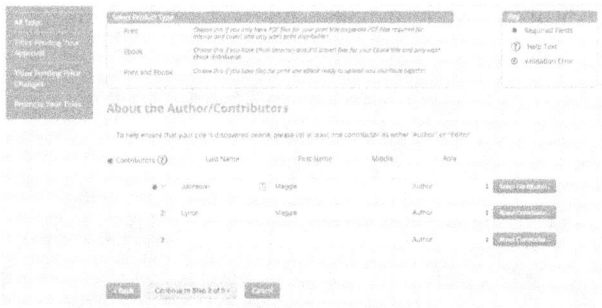

Add Author / Contributor Information

Tip: *When I began writing fiction, I took on two pen name: one for adult novels and one for my YA and Children's books. My real name has always been used for nonfiction. After several requests by my nonfiction readers on how to find my fiction, I realized I was losing out on making it easy for readers, who knew me as Maggie Lynch, to find my fiction titles. A year ago I began adding my real name as a second author to every fiction book. This has served me well* *for potential readers to cross-genres and to provide an easy way readers can see all my titles in one place on vendor sites, even when they use different pen names.*

The third step in the Add Book process is to categorize the title in terms of genre, audience, and physical format. Begin the process by selecting up to three genre categories based on the BISAC identification codes.

First click on the **Find Subjects** button.

This will present a search screen to find the correct BISAC codes. Put the genre category in the search (e.g., romance or mystery or thriller). That will then present you with a list of sub-genre classifications. Choose the classification that most closely matches your book. Repeat this process two more times choosing other genres.

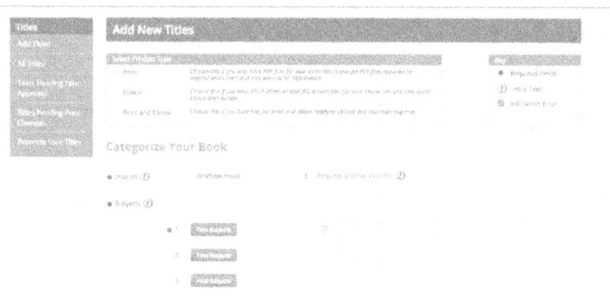

Begin categorizing your title with Find Subject Button

Select	Subject Code	Description
	CGN004090	Comics & Graphic Novels : Romance
	CGN004180	Comics & Graphic Novels : Manga - Romance
	FAM029000	Family & Relationships : Love & Romance
	FIC027000	Fiction : Romance - General
	FIC027010	Fiction : Romance - Erotica
	FIC027020	Fiction : Romance - Contemporary
	FIC027030	Fiction : Romance - Fantasy
	FIC027050	Fiction : Romance - Historical
	FIC027070	Fiction : Romance - Regency
	FIC027080	Fiction : Romance - Short Stories

Identify the best BISAC Code for your title in as narrow category as possible. In this first selection, I chose
Fiction: Romance – Contemporary

NOTE: There are more choices beyond the first displayed screen. Click the page numbers above the display to move to another list of subgenres within the larger genre. For example, in Romance there are 6 pages of selections. This allows you to intelligently pick the best three classifications for your novel.

The remaining categorization options on this screen are not required. However, a few of them may help to add good information to the metadata.

One is the **Regional Subject**. If your book takes place in a particular area (e.g., state, country) you may wish to add that via the Regional Subject. Some readers like to read books that take place in their home state / province. Other readers enjoy reading books about places they have visited or wish to visit like Paris, Iceland, New Zealand, etc.

Skip the Thema classification unless it pertains to you because your country doesn't use BISAC codes. Thema is an alternate classification scheme to BISAC.

Audience is required. Just as described in CreateSpace, the audience for all adult fiction and most nonfiction is Trade, General. If your book is geared toward children (anyone under 19 years old), then make the appropriate age category selection.

Table of Contents is NOT required. However, it is helpful to provide for a nonfiction book to entice readers by the comprehensiveness of the topic presented. If you included that in the long description, there is no need to include it here. The vast majority of fiction does NOT include a Table of Contents section. The one exception may be historical fiction where the book progresses through specific dates or historical events that would be of interest to a potential reader.

Review Quotes section is nice to complete if you have good quotes to share from *known sources*. I rarely complete this section because I don't seek or submit my books to "professional" review sites (e.g., Publisher's Weekly, Kirkus, or New York Review). However, if I have a quote from a well-known USA Today or NYT author, I would include that here. Also include a quote from a reviewer for a well-known genre magazine (e.g., Romantic Times, Ellery Queen, or well-known online review sites).

It is NOT required to include any quotes when loading the book. If you are completing this section, include at least two, but no more than eight review quotes. Below are instructions from Ingram.

✓ Each quote should be brief (no more than 50 words each). Provide excerpts from longer reviews.
  ✓ Separate quotes with a paragraph break.
  ✓ List the most powerful or effective review quote first.

Again click the yellow button at the bottom to continue to the next section, which is **Print Format**.

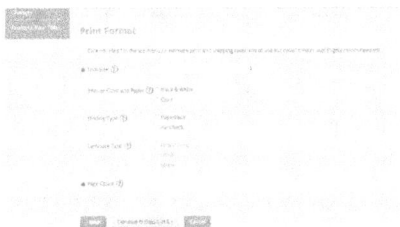

Similar to CreateSpace, this section requires you to detail the trim size (e.g., 6" x 9"). Use dropdown arrow to select. The Interior Color and Paper type, Binding Type, Lamination, and Page Count. The two REQUIRED elements are Trim Size and Page Count. However, you do want to complete the other items in order to get an accurate account of your costs to print each book.

The next section regarding "Print Format" is the ISBN and pricing section.

ISBN. If you are using CreateSpace to ONLY send print books to Amazon (Not choosing Expanded), then you can use the same ISBN at Ingram. However, if you choose Expanded at Amazon AND you are also using Ingram to do worldwide distribution you will want a second ISBN.

I don't recommend using both CreateSpace and Ingram for worldwide distribution because your book will show up twice in all the online catalogs and likely at different pricing. That can be confusing to readers.

Print Format – ISBN and Pricing Section

Pricing. Ingram does not provide automatic conversions of prices across territories. However, it does provide a currency converter tool to help you determine what price you wish to charge in markets outside of your own. I suggest always rounding up the conversion to the 99 cent number (e.g., 7.58 becomes 7.99). In cases where the converted number is below 50 cents (e.g., 12.38) your choice is to round down to 11.99 or up to 12.99. Depending on the country, I often choose to go with the 50 cent designation instead (e.g., 12.50).

Remember, you can change pricing whenever you want. However, populating those prices through all the catalogs worldwide often takes a month to six weeks. So, it is important to put some consideration into the pricing you want.

After the pricing selection, you need to indicate the wholesale discount. As discussed earlier, you can make a choice from as little as 20% to the maximum of 55%. The 55% is the preferred discount for all booksellers and that is what I always choose.

After completing the price and the wholesale discount, Ingram will automatically calculate your profit in each territory.

Publication and On Sale Dates. The publication date is usually the date you are completing the form. The *On Sale Date* is the date you wish it to be available for delivery to customers. Putting the *On Sale Date* or the *Publication Date* in the future is how you indicate this is a Pre-Order product.

Push the next button and you will now see your title on the Dashboard. The next step will be to upload the actual cover file and interior file (PDF). However, before that you will need to provide Publisher Payment information.

Publisher Payment. Before continuing to add your book interior file and cover, you will need to provide some "Publisher Payment" information. Because there are fees associated with setting up a file in Ingram, you must provide a credit or debit card that is on file to assess you those fees as they are incurred.

When you are ready to upload your cover file and interior file, click the yellow CONTINUE button at the bottom of the page. You will then be presented with an opportunity to drag and drop your files, or select them from your computer file manager (finder for Mac).

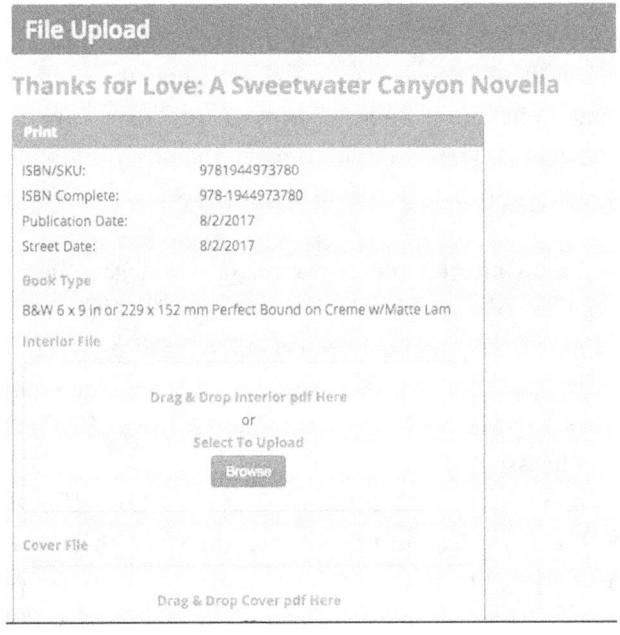

Screen for uploading files to Ingram Spark

As each file is uploaded you will see the uploading progress bar. When the upload is complete, the file name is placed in the box above.

When both the interior and cover files have been uploaded click the CONTINUE button. The files will go through the first step of a two-step validation process. If there are errors, they will be described on the next screen.

What Are Some Typical Errors?

For interior files, Ingram requires the margins to be equal on both the left and right sides. Some templates you may have created or purchased from third parties tend to make the interior margin (the one closest to the binding) larger than the other one. This will create an error.

Two common interior file errors relate to images. One is a color profile problem. This is usually stated as PDF CONTAINS ICC COLOR PROFILES. Ingram prefers all colors to be converted to grayscale for black and white images, or CMYK for color images. Often saving a new PDF with the default setting of PDF/X-1a:2001 will address the issue.

The second common image problem is the LOW RESOLUTION IMAGES IN FILE error. Ingram recommends that images be a minimum of 300 ppi (pixels per inch) and line art at 600 ppi. This often happens when an author includes images retrieved from the Internet. Images for display on a computer tend to be compressed and have a lower ppi of 72-120. I have found that the minimum acceptable quality is about 225 ppi, though 300 is certainly better. It is always best to get the maximum density possible for the most clear images.

Ingram will let you continue even with these errors, but they warn you that the images may not be of good quality in the printed book. You will be able to check them in the PDF proof and make a decision before putting it on sale or getting it printed.

Cover File Errors tend to be around the size of the spine. As discussed earlier, the spine size is calculated based on the total number of pages in the book. The total pages must be divisible by two, as they are printed front to back. When you have completed your book, the total page number includes ALL pages—copyright page, front matter, back matter, blank pages, as well as the primary content. A difference of even five pages can make a difference in the spine size. Too small of a spine and the pages are stuffed, making the binding more likely to break. Too big of a spine and the pages are too lose for the glue to hold them well, again providing more opportunities for the spine to break.

Tip: *Don't have the full wrap cover done before you have the final interior copy completed.*

When I first began publishing my books in print, I would get the cover designed in advance for both print and ebook (usually a savings) in order to use it in pre-launch marketing. The problem with that is that I had to estimate the spine size based on what I thought the finished novel would be. Believe me, I was NEVER exactly right. Sometimes I wrote longer, sometimes shorter. Sometimes I decided to add a sneak peek of another book or add extra back matter that added pages to the book and therefore changed the spine size.

Though a designer can go back in and change the spine, it is not usually a simple change. Frequently, in addition to the book title and author name, the spine has some continuation of the primary background image that flows from front cover to back cover. How that lines up with a 1" spine is different from how it lines up with a ¾" spine or a ½" spine. In other words, that change will cost you.

Now I just use the front cover for marketing of upcoming releases —whether in print or ebook. Then when I know the print book interior content is finalized, I send the page count to my cover designer and she does the full wrap at that time.

Final Step in Ingram Upload Process

Once you have confirmed the uploaded files, after the initial online verification of those files, they are sent for the second level verification which involves creating the print-ready PDF file. If you chose to go ahead in spite of errors, a person may look at the file and contact you if he/she believes those errors will significantly compromise the quality of your book.

You will also have an opportunity to look at the final print-ready PDF file. You must approve it before your book is actually made available for print and the data sent to all their distribution partners. If you prefer to look at a physical proof copy of your book, you may order one to review prior to approving the book for sale. The cost is the sum of your printing cost (e.g., $4.00) plus the cost to ship the book to your home. Typically that total is about $8.00-$10 with standard (3 day) shipping.

One final thing to consider when working with Ingram. Once you have put your book on sale, if you find ANYTHING you want to change, there will be a $25 change fee.

Authors who are used to the ebook world of making changes whenever you want at no cost (CreateSpace also does not charge for changes), may not take the time needed to make sure the interior files are truly finalized. Far too many authors get excited about getting their book created in print form, then decide to give it a final read *after* they get their first print copy or a box of print books they ordered. Inevitably, they find typos or grammar errors or other problems and want to change it and put it back up again. You CAN do that, but there is a $25 fee.

I've seen some others do that three or four times and easily run up $100 in change fees because they didn't catch something the first time.

Beware of how your proofing process may need to be modified if you don't want additional bills at Ingram Spark.

Book Now on Sale

Once you have approved the PROOF PDF or Physical Book Proof, your book is then set for sale. Just as in the Expanded version of CreateSpace, it takes up to 6 weeks for it to be available in the catalogs all eligible distribution partners around the world. The larger booksellers (e.g., Barnes and Noble, Books-a-Million, Powells) tend to have it within about two weeks. However, smaller independent bookstores often don't have it for a month in their catalog.

If you are planning some big launch marketing for your print book, beware of the availability process. You don't want hundreds or thousands of readers excited to purchase the book and it is only available on one or two sites.

Chapter Six
NEXT STEPS

Now that you have the tools to both publish your manuscript and get it distributed around the world, you need to put together a good book launch and design an ongoing marketing plan. Marketing beyond the launch is critical to having a more regular monthly income. If you put all of your marketing effort in the launch, you will find a steep drop off within a few weeks after the book is released.

You can learn how to do that through the book *Secrets of Effective Author Marketing*. Finally, if you want to make writing and publishing your career, check out *Secrets to Building the Career You Want*.

Need a little more handholding and mentoring with these steps? Please check out my online Indie Publishing Series at AWW on the Go: http://aww-on-the-go.teachable.com/ These courses are available for you to move through at your own pace. Begin with the FREE courses on the basics, then decide what other skills you need for additional courses.

These courses provide additional handouts, cheat sheets, one-on-one discussions and troubleshooting through a private Facebook group, as well as live web-conference demonstrations and coaching sessions a couple of times a year.

Did You Find This Book Helpful?

If you did, I would really appreciate a short review on any platform you frequent—Goodreads, Amazon, Kobo, Nook, and Apple. Reviews are the best way that authors have to share their books with others.

Want to Keep in Touch and Know When New Books are Available?

Join my mailing list just for authors and I will send you the first book in my Career Author Secrets series for free. You can learn more here: https://app.convertkit.com/landing_pages/93200?v=6

ABOUT THE AUTHOR

Maggie is the author of 20+ published books, as well as more than 60 short stories and numerous non-fiction articles. She is also the founder of Windtree Press, an independent publishing cooperative. Her love of lifelong-learning has garnered degrees in psychology, counseling, computer science, and education; and led to opportunities to consult in Europe, Australia, and the Middle East. Since 2013, Maggie has enjoyed the luxury of writing full-time. Her adult fiction spans romance, suspense, and SF titles under the name Maggie Jaimeson. She writes YA Fantasy under the name Maggie Faire. Her non-fiction titles are found under Maggie McVay Lynch.

For more information contact Maggie at:
maggielynch.com
maggie@maggielynch.com

Visit us at http://windtreepress.com

www.ingramcontent.com/pod-product-compliance
Lightning Source LLC
Chambersburg PA
CBHW071734080526
44588CB00013B/2029